FOCKE-WULF

J. Richard Smith

Focke-Wulf
AN AIRCRAFT ALBUM

No. 6

Arco Publishing Company, Inc.
NEW YORK

Published by ARCO PUBLISHING
COMPANY, INC.
219 Park Avenue South,
New York, N.Y. 10003

First published 1973

© Ian Allan, 1973

Library of Congress Catalog Card
Number 73-81386

ISBN 0-668-03349-5

Printed in Great Britain

ACKNOWLEDGEMENTS
I should like to record my grateful thanks to
H. J. Nowarra who supplied a large number of
photographs and some information to help
make this book a reality. Thanks are also due
to Antony L. Kay for his help with the helicopter section of this book and to Ian Prim-
mer, Thomas H. Hitchcock, Deutsche Lufthansa, and H. J. Meier of Vereinigte Flugtechnische Werke for their various contribu-
tions. Last, but not least, I would like to thank
my good friend Eddie Creek who supplied
several previously unpublished photos.

PHOTO CREDITS
Eddie Creek: pages 48 (top), 49 (top), 51
(top), 54 (left), 55 (left), 56, 57, 58, 59, 60
(left), 63 (bottom), 64, 66 (bottom), 68
(right), 70, 71, 72, 74 (bottom), 77, 88 (top),
89, 90, 99, 101.
Lufthansa: pages 15 (bottom), 25, 9 (top).
Nowarra: Frontispiece and pages 7, 8, 9
(bottom), 10, 12, 13, 14, 15 (top), 16, 17
(top), 18, 19, 20, 21, 22, 23, 24, 26 (left), 27,
28, 33, 34, 37, 38, 40 (right), 41, 42, 43, 46,
49 (bottom), 50, 51 (bottom), 52, 54 (right),
55 (right), 61, 62, 63 (top), 73, 74 (top), 76
(right), 78, 79 (left), 80, 81 (top), 82, 83, 84,
85, 86, 87, 88 (bottom), 93, 94, 95, 96, 97,
102, 103, 104, 106, 108, 109.
H. Obert via Eddie Creek: pages 67, 68 (left).
Alfred Price: page 81 (bottom).
Real Photos: pages 17 (bottom), 26 (right),
29, 30, 31, 35, 36, 39 (top), 44, 45, 53, 75,
76 (left), 98.
Harold Thiele: page 32.
Via Eddie Creek: page 11.
Jaroslav Zazvonil: pages 47, 48 (bottom), 65,
66 (top), 100.

Contents

Introduction *page* 7
Aeroplane Types 12
A 7 Storch 12
A 16 12
S 1 14
S 2 14
A 17 Möwe 15
GL 18 16
F 19 Ente 17
A 20 Habicht 19
A 21 19
GL 22 20
W 4 20
S 24 Kiebitz 21
A 26 22
A 28 Habicht 23
A 29 Möwe 23
A 32 Bussard 24
A 33 Sperber 25
A 36 26
A 38 Möwe 26

A 39 *page* 27
A 40 27
W 7 28
Fw 43 Falke 29
Fw 44 Stieglitz 29
Fw 47 32
S 48 34
Fw 55 34
Fw 56 Stösser 35
Fw 57 37
Fw 58 Weihe 38
Fw 62 41
Fw 159 42
Fw 187 Falke 44
Fw 189 Uhu 46
Fw 190A 51
Fw 190B and C 61
Fw 190D 62
Fw 190F and G 64
Fw 191 70
Fw 200 Condor 71

Ta 152 and Ta 153 *page* 82
Ta 154 87
Ta 183 91
Rotating Wing Aircraft 93
C 19 Don Quichote 93
C 30 Heuschrecke 94
Fw 61 94
Fw 186 97
Fa 266 Hornisse 97
Fa 223 Drache 98
Fa 224 Libelle 101
Fa 225 102
Fa 284 102
Fa 330 Bachstelze 103
Wartime Aircraft Projects 104
VAK 191B 107
VFW 614 108
Some Notes on Aircraft and Unit
  Designations 109
Abbreviations 110
Type and Production List 111

Frontispiece: *The VAK 191B which made its First Flight on September 10th, 1971.*

Introduction

On October 8th, 1890, some thirteen years before the first sustained flight by the Wright brothers, a son was born to Dr Johann Focke, an influential member of the Bremen Senate in Northern Germany. Named Heinrich Karl Johann, the son was to have a considerable influence on the world of aviation, particularly in the field of helicopter development.

As early as December 1908, Heinrich's elder brother Wilhelm had patented a design for a pusher type aeroplane. The machine was completed in September 1909, but only succeeded in making short ground hops. One of Wilhelm's designs was built successfully by the Rumpler company later in 1909, whilst Heinrich turned his attentions to the construction of a small glider.

After gathering together more funds, the brothers built another pusher aircraft powered by an 8hp NSU engine given to them by Oscar Müller, but this failed to leave the ground. Heinrich, with a friend named Kolthoff, then began work on a more conventional monoplane with the same NSU engine mounted in the nose driving a tractor airscrew. Despite its promise, the machine, designated A 4, failed to leave the ground owing to its low engine power.

It was at this time that Georg Wulf, a young 17-year-old apprentice, joined Heinrich Focke and Kolthoff in their aeronautical activities. Lack of success with the A 4 led to the friends appealing to Oscar Müller for a more powerful engine. Eventually he supplied them with a new 50hp Argus four-cylinder in-line engine which, although very welcome, forced a complete redesign of the aircraft. The new machine, designated A 5, was of the familiar 'Taube' type, a mid-wing monoplane with a fixed, four-wheel undercarriage and a single open cockpit.

The Focke A 5 made its first flight late in 1912 with Kolthoff at the controls. From then on it was extensively tested, suffering minor crashes and being repaired again and again. Georg Wulf taught himself to fly in the single-seat machine and eventually became a competent pilot. When World War I was declared in August 1914, both Focke and Wulf eventually joined the German Army Air Service, although the former suffered a severe crash in 1916 at Seraincourt near Rheims.

After the war, Focke and Wulf began the construction of another aircraft, the A 7 *Storch*, and such was its success that a group of Bremen businessmen, led by Dr Ludwig Roselius, owner of the famous Kaffee-Hag company, contributed 200,000 RM towards the establishment of an aircraft building enterprise. Known as the Focke-Wulf Flugzeugbau AG, the company was formed on January 1st, 1924 with Heinrich Focke as Technical Director, Georg Wulf as test pilot and Dr Werner Naumann as Commercial Director.

The company's first real success was the Focke-Wulf A 16 which was built in a hanger shared with the Deutsche Aero Lloyd airline, predecessor of Lufthansa. Despite a series of financial crises and the death of Georg Wulf whilst flying the F 19 *Ente* in September 1927, the company managed to survive and produce a number of successful aircraft including the *Möwe* series of airliners and the S 24 *Kiebitz* lightplane.

Perhaps the year 1931 was the most momentous for the young Focke-Wulf

The unsuccessful Focke A 4 which failed to leave the ground owing to the low power of its NSU engine.

The A5 was the first aircraft designed by Heinrich Focke to fly successfully.

company. When the year began it had 150 employees, was virtually unknown outside Germany, and then was frequently confused with the Dutch Fokker company with which it had no connection. Early in the year, Focke, now a Professor, set up a separate section inside the company to study rotary wing aircraft, acquiring permission to build the Cievra 19 autogyro under licence. As Focke became more and more engrossed in rotary wing flight, it was obvious that a new conventional aircraft designer would have to be appointed. Therefore, on November 1st, 1931 a young engineer was acquired from BFW, Kurt Waldemar Tank.

Kurt Tank was born on February 24th, 1898 in Bromberg-Schwedenhöhe but in 1905 his family moved to Nakel on the River Netze. Even at this age, Tank was fascinated by the shape of fish and the way they smoothly steered themselves through the water. In 1919 Tank took an electrical engineering course at Berlin Technical High School receiving his diploma in 1924. During his time at the school he formed, with a number of friends, the Akaflieg Berlin, a section of enthusiasts dedicated to the design and construction of gliders. Rejected by the Albatros company, Tank's first glider, named *Teufelchen* (Little Devil) after his bride to be, Charlotte Teufel, was eventually built by the LFG GmbH at Stralsund.

After graduating, Tank joined the Rohrbach company at Berlin-Staaken. Although virtually unknown today, the Rohrbach Metallflugzeugbau GmbH pioneered all-metal aircraft structures with smooth (as opposed to the corrugated surfaces designed by Junkers) metal covering. Tank's first task was to redesign the hull of the Ro IIA flying boat, producing the Ro IIIA *Rodra* which was an immediate success.

The first Rohrbach machine to be designed entirely by Tank was the *Robbe* I, a flying boat developed from the *Rodra*. This was followed by the Ro V *Rocco*, the Ro VII *Robbe* II and the Ro X *Romar* flying boats and the Ro VIII *Roland*, a landplane version of the *Romar*. Because of the restrictions on aircraft development in Germany under the Treaty of Versailles, many early Rohrbach aircraft were built by a sister company in Copenhagen.

The twin-engined *Rocco* and three-engined *Romar* and *Roland* were all used by Lufthansa, some serving with the airline until 1936. An interesting part of the original *Roland* design was its extensively glazed cockpit which Tank had designed. This radical feature was originally rejected by Lufthansa officials, but after the inauguration of a service from Munich to Milan over the Alps, several aviators, including Hans Baur (later to become Hitler's personal pilot) complained about the intense cold. Tank was quick to point out that he had already designed and built a solution to the problem. All *Rolands* were subsequently fitted with cockpit canopies.

The last design produced by Tank for Rohrbach was the Ro IX *Rofix* all-metal fighter monoplane built in 1927 and flown in Copenhagen. By 1929, the Rohrbach company was beginning to experience financial difficulties and Tank left the

firm to join BFW at Augsburg. His stay
was too short to have any lasting influence
on the design of Messerschmitt aircraft,
and by November 1931 he had moved to
Focke-Wulf at Bremen.

By the end of 1931, with the recession in
world markets, many aircraft companies
in Germany were approaching bankruptcy. Apart from Rohrbach which has
already been mentioned, BFW filed a
bankruptcy petition in June 1931, Henschel
attempted to take over the tottering
Junkers organisation and Focke-Wulf
amalgamated with the Albatros Flugzeugwerke GmbH of Berlin.

Focke-Wulf took over many personnel
and the L 75, L 84, L 101, L 102 and L 103
designs from Albatros which it continued
to build. The success of the new A 44
Stieglitz (later Fw 44) trainer did much to
improve the fortunes of the company,
which now began to become known outside Germany. One of the first aircraft
designed by Tank, the Fw 56 *Stösser*
proved a great success as did the twin-
engined Fw 58 *Weihe* communications
aircraft. Towards the end of 1933, Heinrich
Focke left the company to establish his own
rotorcraft factory at Hoyenkamp near
Bremen known as the Focke-Achgelis
GmbH. Tank immediately took over as
Technical Director of Focke-Wulf.

With the advent of the Nazi regime, the
activities of the German aircraft companies
experienced a dramatic upsurge. Focke-
Wulf were given several contracts for the

*Top right: The L 73 airliner was typical of
Albatros aircraft of the late '20s and early '30s.*

*Bottom right: Professor Kurt Tank in the cockpit
of his most famous product, the Focke-
Wulf 190.*

The Rohrbach Romar twin-engined flying boat was one of the aircraft developed by Kurt Tank before he joined Focke-Wulf.

licence production of military aircraft for the fledgeling Luftwaffe, and in June 1936 was reformed as the Focke-Wulf Flugzeugbau GmbH with capital provided by the huge AEG electrical combine, into whose control it passed.

By 1938, the company had a capital of 2½ million RM and had built the first of the remarkable series of *Condor* airliners. It was this aircraft more than any other that established Focke-Wulf abroad; making several long-distance flights to remote parts of the world. When the war began, the company was still building aircraft under licence including the Bf 109 and Bf 110 fighters, but, in 1941, production switched to the Fw 190.

Undoubtedly the most successful aircraft produced by the company, the Fw 190 was little short of a masterpiece. When it made its operational debut in 1941 it at last broke the superiority which the RAF had gained with the Spitfire, and served with the Luftwaffe until the end of the war, eventually becoming known as the Ta 152. Apart from the Fw 189, Fw 190 and *Condor*, Focke-Wulf failed to contribute any other aircraft to the war effort. However a number of fascinating advanced designs did flow from the project office. These included the Ta 400 bomber, the Ta 183 jet fighter, the Ta 283 ramjet fighter and the *Triebflügel* vertical take-off project. By the end of the war, Focke-Wulf, with its sub-contractors, employed 28,960 personnel.

On April 8th, 1945 British forces captured the Focke-Wulf plant at Bad Eilsen near Buckeburg. Apart from the design office, the British also captured Kurt Tank, then one of the most famous aircraft designers in the world. After intensive interrogation, Tank received offers from many countries to help in developing their aircraft industries. In particular the Russians were most interested in his work, having captured many of the detailed drawings for the Ta 183 from the DVL centre at Berlin-Adlershof.

Whilst all these negotiations were taking place, Tank began work on an extremely advanced jet airliner project which he designated Ta 500. The Ta 500 was to carry 30 passengers over a distance of

6,000 miles at a cruising speed of 590 miles per hour. It was to be powered by five Rolls-Royce Nene turbojets, carry a crew of four and have a service ceiling of 58,000ft.

Eventually, in 1947, Tank received a firm offer from the Argentine government of President Peron. Travelling in the utmost secrecy under the name of 'Peter Matties', Tank arrived in Buenos Aires via Copenhagen. Here he joined the Industrias Aeronauticas y Meccanicas del Estado (IAME) company of Cordoba.

The Focke-Wulf company was resurrected in Germany, undertaking the licence production of several aircraft including the Kranich glider in 1951, the BL–502 lightplane in 1957 and the Piaggio P–149D in the same year. During 1963 the Focke-Wulf GmbH and the Weser Flugzeugbau GmbH combined to form the Vereinigte Flugtechnische Werke with headquarters in Bremen.

In January 1965 the Heinkel company joined the newly established corporation and during the winter of 1969/70 a merger was arranged between the Royal Netherlands Aircraft Factory and VFW under the designation Zentralgesellschaft VFW–Fokker GmbH. With headquarters at Düsseldorf, the new company has approximately 20,000 employees and is responsible for the F 27 Friendship, the F 28 Fellowship and VFW 614 airliners and the VAK 191B vertical take-off aircraft.

Aeroplane Types

A 7 Storch

After the end of World War I, Heinrich Focke and Georg Wulf again joined forces to continue the construction of aircraft. Their first post-war venture was a neat mid-wing monoplane built of wood, with wood and fabric covering, powered by a 50hp Argus engine. The tandem two-seat design was fitted with a fixed, braced undercarriage and had a crash pylon mounted above the forward cockpit.

Construction of the aircraft, designated A 7 *Storch* (Stork), began in a Bremen cellar but was temporarily halted pending investigation by the Inter Allied Control Commission. After examination by a French officer, construction was allowed to continue, and was eventually completed towards the end of 1921. In November Georg Wulf took the aircraft up on its first flight, subsequently attaining an altitude of 650ft. The aircraft was later badly damaged on the ground by a severe storm.

It was not until the summer of 1922 that the A 7 (almost certainly given the *Werke Nummer* 1) was rebuilt, the airframe being fitted with a 55hp Siemens Sh 10 five-cylinder radial. In December the machine was registered D–264 and allocated a German passenger licence. A demonstration of the aircraft in 1923 before Wulf's tutor, Professor Proell, led to a group of Bremen businessmen becoming interested in the work of the two airmen, and the eventual creation of the Focke-Wulf company.

Specification

POWERPLANT	1 × 55hp Siemens Sh 10 radial
SPAN	14.00m (45ft 11¼in)
LENGTH	8.40m (27ft 6¾in)
WEIGHT EMPTY	440kg (970lb)
WEIGHT LOADED	630kg (1,389lb)
MAX SPEED	100km/h (62mph)
SERVICE CEILING	3,000m (9,843ft)

Focke and Wulf's first post-war venture was the A 7. Only one aircraft (D–264–w/nr 1) was completed.

A 16

The first product of the newly created Focke-Wulf Flugzeugbau AG was the A 16 light airliner. A neat shoulder-wing monoplane, the A16 was built entirely of wood with plywood covering. The wing was of thick Zanonia-form construction, with straight leading and curved trailing edges. The ailerons, the chord of which increased towards the tips, were fixed at an angle to the tailing edge of the wing. This type of wing, first tested by the A 7 *Storch* was subsequently fitted to many other Focke-Wulf aircraft.

The A16 had a deep section fuselage with an enclosed cabin for three or four passengers. The pilot sat in an open cockpit cut into the leading edge of the wing, and the mainwheels were mounted on small cantilever struts attached to the bottom of the fuselage.

On June 23rd, 1924 the prototype A 16 (w/nr 2) made its first flight with Georg Wulf at the controls. The machine was powered by a 75hp Siemens Sh 11 seven-cylinder radial driving a two-bladed airscrew. Within three days the aircraft had reached a speed of 84mph with four people on board, and was later registered D–437.

The second aircraft, D–467 (w/nr 3) was delivered to Bremer Luftverkehr AG on July 13th, 1924 and used to inaugurate a service from Bremen to Wangerooge in the East Friesian Islands. The company also operated D–647 (w/nr 4) which was powered by a 100hp Mercedes engine as the A 16a.

Eventually five production variants were constructed; the A 16 powered by a 75hp Siemens Sh 11, the A 16a with the 100hp

Mercedes D I six-cylinder in-line, the A 16b with the 85hp Junkers L 1a eight-cylinder in-line, the A 16c with the 100hp Siemens Sh 12 nine-cylinder radial and the A 16d with the 120hp Mercedes D II or D IIa six-cylinder in-line.

Apart from D-533 and D-646 about which little is known, there were three A 16as, all of which were converted to A 16cs or ds. Two A 16bs were built, both (D-658 and D-659) being delivered initially to Junkers Luftverkehr. The last named aircraft was later bought by the newspaper company Berliner Lokal Anzeiger and finally transferred to Lufthansa and named *Borkum*. Four Focke-Wulf A 16cs were also used by Lufthansa including D-467 *Westerland*, D-647 *Hansa*, D-548 (w/nr 5) *Baden* and D-814 (w/nr 7) *Wangerooge*.

The main production variant however was the A 16d of which at least nine aircraft were built or converted. These included six; D-671, D-747, D-804, D-895, D-916 and D-959 (w/nrs 10, 11, 12, 24, 25 and 26 respectively) owned by Luftverkehr AG Niedersachsen. The other three A 16ds; D-162, D-763 and D-1129 were delivered to LVG Wilhelmshaven-Rüstringen, Flugverkehr Halle AG and Luftverkehr AG Westfalen. Two aircraft (D-566 and D-914) were delivered to the DVS, the remaining machine (D-731 w/nr 9) going to Norddeutsche Luftverkehr.

Specification

	A16	A16a	A16b
SPAN	13.90m (45ft 7¼in)	13.90m (45ft 7¼in)	13.90m (45ft 7¼in)
LENGTH	8.50m (27ft 10¾in)	9.10m (29ft 10¼in)	9.10m (29ft 10¼in)
HEIGHT	2.30m (7ft 6½in)	2.30m (7ft 6½in)	2.30m (7ft 6½in)
WEIGHT EMPTY	570kg (1,256lb)	760kg (1,675lb)	570kg (1,256lb)
WEIGHT LOADED	970kg (2,138lb)	1,201kg (2,647lb)	970kg (2,138lb)
MAX SPEED	135km/h (84mph)	145km/h (90mph)	135km/h (84mph)
SERVICE CEILING	2,500m (8,202ft)	3,000m (9,842ft)	2,500m (8,202ft)
NORMAL RANGE	550km (341 miles)	500km (310 miles)	550km (341 miles)

S 1

In 1925 Focke-Wulf began work on a pair of two-seat training and sporting aircraft developed from the A 7 *Storch*. These two machines, the Focke-Wulf S 1 and S 2, were unusual for the period in having the seats mounted side-by-side, a feature now generally considered useful for training aircraft.

The Focke-Wulf S 1 was a shoulder-wing monoplane built of wood with mixed plywood and fabric covering. The wing was of typical Zanonia-form with the ailerons hinged to the trailing edge. The fixed undercarriage was braced to the lower fuselage longerons by V-struts and a small tailskid was fitted. The original aircraft was powered by an uncowled Siemens Sh 5 five-cylinder air-cooled radial engine which produced 55hp for take-off.

A later conversion, the S 1a, was powered by a Junkers L 1 eight-cylinder in-line engine which developed 75hp for take-off. This variant was slightly heavier than the S 1, and had an improved maximum speed of 140km/h (87mph). Probably only one or two Focke-Wulf S 1s were built, one of these being registered D–820. The type was delivered to a DVS training school during 1926 where it saw limited service.

Specification (S 1)

POWERPLANT	1 × 55hp Siemens Sh 5 radial
SPAN	12.00m (39ft 4½in)
LENGTH	8.10m (26ft 7in)
HEIGHT	2.30m (7ft 6½in)
WEIGHT EMPTY	470kg (1,036lb)
WEIGHT LOADED	670kg (1,477lb)
MAX SPEED	130km/h (81mph)
SERVICE CEILING	3,000 (9,842ft)
NORMAL RANGE	350km (217 miles)

S 2

The Focke-Wulf S 2 was a development of the S 1 produced in 1927. Employing the same fuselage and undercarriage as the S 1, the S 2 differed in having a parasol wing supported by a complicated series of N- and V-section struts. The aircraft was powered by an uncowled 80hp Siemens Sh 11 seven-cylinder air-cooled radial driving a two-bladed wooden airscrew. Like the S 1, the only S 2 to be completed was delivered to a DVS training school in 1928.

Specification

POWERPLANT	1 × 80hp Siemens Sh 11 radial
SPAN	12.00m (39ft 4½in)
LENGTH	8.10m (26ft 7in)
HEIGHT	2.80m (9ft 2½in)
WEIGHT EMPTY	570kg (1,256lb)
WEIGHT LOADED	820kg (1,808lb)
MAX SPEED	135km/h (84mph)
SERVICE CEILING	3,500m (11,482ft)
NORMAL RANGE	480km (298 miles)

Left: *The Focke-Wulf S 1 was a development of the A 7 designed as a primary trainer. It was unusual for aircraft of the period in having two seats positioned side by side.*

Top right: *Bearing some similarity to the Focke-Wulf S 1, the S 2 had a parasol wing.*

Bottom right: *The prototype A 17a Möwe in service with Lufthansa as D–1149 Bremen. The aircraft was originally delivered to Norddeutsche Luftverkehr for use on their Bremen services.*

A 17 Möwe

The Focke-Wulf A 17 was the first of a series of successful light airliners and transports produced by the company under the generic name of *Möwe* (Seagull). The A 17 was basically an enlarged and improved A 16 with a wing of similar planform built of wood with plywood covering. The fuselage was constructed of welded steel tube with plywood covering to the rear of the cabin area and fabric aft. Provision was made for eight to nine passengers, with a crew of two housed in a fully glazed cockpit. The single mainwheels were attached to the fuselage by V struts and braced to the underside of the wing by I section struts and a fixed tailskid was provided.

The prototype A 17, D–1149 (w/nr 32) made its first flight in 1927 powered by a 420hp Gnome Rhone Jupiter 9Ab nine-cylinder radial engine. It was delivered to the airline Norddeutsche Luftverkehr in 1928 and eventually passed to Lufthansa with the name *Bremen*.

Eleven production aircraft were completed, these differing mainly in having increased rudder area. Several aircraft were fitted with a 480hp Siemens Jupiter radial under the designation A 17a, and one machine, D–1444 *Münster* (w/nr 50), was fitted with a 520hp Junkers Jumo 5 heavy oil engine as the A 17c.

Of the 11 production A 17s completed, w/nrs 42 to 51 (respectively D–1342 *Emden*, D–1358 *Aurich*, D–1367 *Leer*, D–1380 *Oldenburg*, D–1388 *Stade*, D–1403 *Lüneburg*, D–1416 *Osnabruck*, D–1430 *Hannover*, D–1444 *Münster* and D–1484 *Bielefeld*) were delivered to Lufthansa who

15

used them on their Berlin–Cologne and Cologne–Nuremburg services. The other aircraft, D–1345 (w/nr 38) was used successively by the DVL, the Albatros company and the DVS. Two aircraft, D–1430 and D–1444 were later re-registered D–UTOS and D–UNIK respectively.

Specification

POWERPLANT	1 × 480hp Siemens Jupiter radial
SPAN	20.00m (65ft 7¼in)
LENGTH	14.63m (48ft 0in)
HEIGHT	3.20m (10ft 6in)
WEIGHT EMPTY	2,450kg (5,401lb)
WEIGHT LOADED	4,000kg (8,818lb)
MAX SPEED	201km/h (125mph)
SERVICE CEILING	4,500m (14,763ft)
NORMAL RANGE	800km (497 miles)

GL 18

The first of only three twin-engined aeroplanes designed by Heinrich Focke, the GL 18 was basically a modified A 16 powered by two 78hp Junkers L 1a in-line engines in circular cowlings. Like the A 16, the GL 18 was built of wood throughout, the single forward mounted engine being replaced by a neatly faired nose. The engines of the GL 18 were partly buried in the wing leading edges, each driving a two-bladed airscrew.

The GL 18a made its first flight on August 9th, 1926, one aircraft, D–967 *Helgoland* (w/nr 28) being subsequently delivered to Lufthansa. A modified version of the design was also built designated GL 18c. This differed in having a wider section fuselage and being powered by two 110hp Siemens Sh 12 radials. The GL 18, which was used as a crew trainer and light transport, was only built in very small numbers.

Specification (GL 18a)

POWERPLANTS	2 × 78hp Junkers L 1a in-lines
SPAN	16.00m (52ft 6in)
LENGTH	8.50m (27ft 10¾in)
HEIGHT	2.60m (8ft 6⅓in)
WEIGHT EMPTY	925kg (2,040lb)
WEIGHT LOADED	1,450kg (3,197lb)
MAX SPEED	135km/h (84mph)
SERVICE CEILING	3,400m (11,155ft)

Only one Focke-Wulf A 17c was completed, the type differing in being powered by a Jumo 5 heavy oil engine.

The Focke-Wulf GL 18 was basically a twin-engined version of the A 16.

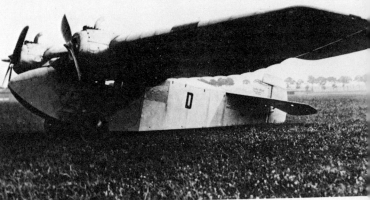

Only one Focke-Wulf GL 18c was completed, this variant differing in being powered by two Siemens Sh 12 radials.

The unusual F 19a Ente light transport, the earlier variant in which Georg Wulf lost his life on September 29th, 1927.

F 19 Ente

Although only two aircraft were built, the F 19 *Ente* (Duck) represented an important milestone in the history of Focke-Wulf. Even before World War I, Wilhelm Focke, Heinrich's elder brother, had worked on the design of tail-first or Canard aircraft. Eventually one of his designs was built by the Rumpler Flugzeugwerke in 1909. Powered by a 40hp Argus engine, the aircraft was successfully flown at Berlin-Johannisthal in September.

In 1925 Heinrich Focke resurrected the idea of a tail-first aircraft, submitting proposals for the F 19 *Ente* to the DVL. The F 19 was a neat shoulder wing monoplane with a conventional fin and rudder, but with the stabiliser mounted above the nose on a large supporting strut. The fuselage was built of welded steel tube with fabric covering and its open cockpit contained two seats, two additional seats being provided in the tiny cabin. The wings and foreplane were built of plywood with fabric covering, the span of each surface being 45ft 11¼in and 17ft 0¾in respectively. The mainwheel legs were attached to the underside of the wings and braced to the fuselage sides, and a semi-enclosed nosewheel was positioned below and just forward of the cockpit. The F 19 was powered by two 75hp Siemens Sh 11 seven-cylinder radial engines mounted below the wings driving two-bladed airscrews.

After wind tunnel tests at Göttingen, construction of the F 19 prototype began at Focke-Wulf's Bremen factory. On September 2nd, 1927, *Ober Ing* Georg Wulf took the aircraft up on its maiden flight. Fourteen successful tests followed, but on

September 29th, whilst demonstrating the aircraft's single-engine capabilities, the F 19 suddenly spun into the ground and crashed, killing Georg Wulf. Subsequent investigation showed that a broken control rod had caused the death of Wulf and not the radical layout of the design.

Despite the tragedy of Wulf's death, Focke continued the development of the *Ente*, producing the improved F 19a towards the end of 1930. This had considerably reduced wing span, and two auxiliary wire-braced vertical stabilisers attached below the wing outboard of the engine nacelles. The F 19a (registered D–1960) made its first flight late in 1930, with Cornelius Edzard at the controls.

Successful test flights led to the grant of a German passenger-carrying certificate and subsequent demonstration flights were made in Germany and Denmark. In 1931, the F 19a was flown to Britain, and was also demonstrated in Holland and Belgium during the following year. Despite its unblemished flying record, no production orders for the F 19a were forthcoming, and the sole aircraft was used as a test vehicle by the DVL at Berlin-Adlershof until 1939.

Specification (F 19a)

POWERPLANTS	2 × 110hp Siemens Sh 14 radials
SPAN	10.00m (32ft 9½in)
LENGTH	10.53m (34ft 6½in)
HEIGHT	4.15m (13ft 7⅓in)
WEIGHT EMPTY	1,175kg (2,590lb)
WEIGHT LOADED	1,650kg (3,638lb)
MAX SPEED	142km/h (88mph)
SERVICE CEILING	3,000m (9,842ft)

18

A 20 Habicht

The Focke-Wulf A 20 *Habicht* (Hawk) was a development of the A 16 airliner and transport. It was a high-wing monoplane with a wooden Zanonia-form wing and a square section fuselage of mixed construction. Fabric covering was used throughout and the single mainwheels were braced to the lower part of the fuselage and the underside of the wing.

Construction of the A 20 began in 1927, the first aircraft, D–1159 (w/nr 34) being powered by a 120hp Daimler D IIa six-cylinder liquid-cooled in-line engine. The pilot was seated below the leading edge of the wing in an enclosed cockpit, and provision was made for three or four passengers in a small cabin. The first aircraft, which was later registered D–OFOR, was delivered to Deutsche Verkehrsflug and used mainly on the company's Augsburg–Nuremberg route. Two other aircraft were completed, D–1439 (w/nr 53) delivered to

Luftverkehrsgesellschaft Wilhelmshaven–Rüstringen and D–1726 (w/nr 94) used by a private owner L. Monheim.

During 1928, a development of the *Habicht* was completed under the designation A 20a. The variant differed mainly in being powered by a 200hp Siemens-built Wright Whirlwind air-cooled radial engine and having increased wing area. Only one A 20a was completed, registered D–1482 (w/nr 52).

Specification (A 20)

POWERPLANT	One 120hp Daimler D IIa in-line
SPAN	16.00m (52ft 6in)
LENGTH	10.20m (33ft 5½in)
HEIGHT	3.00m (9ft 10in)
WEIGHT EMPTY	1,025kg (2,259lb)
WEIGHT LOADED	1,425kg (3,141lb)
MAX SPEED	145km/h (90mph)
SERVICE CEILING	3,500m (11,482ft)
NORMAL RANGE	600km (373 miles)

A 21

The Focke-Wulf A 21 was a development of the A 17 *Möwe* intended for use as a specialised photographic and aerial mapping aircraft. Produced late in 1927, the airframe of the A 21 was similar to that of the A 17, but a large square opening was made in the fuselage side, between the first and last cabin window. This was to allow for ease of observation and the use of hand-held cameras. Apart from this, the A 21 also differed in being powered by a 450hp BMW VI twelve-cylinder in-line engine.

Probably intended for use by Hansa Luftbild, the German aerial mapping company, only one prototype of the A 21 was completed.

Specification

POWERPLANT	1 × 450hp BMW VI in-line
SPAN	20.00m (65ft 7½in)
LENGTH	13.00m (42ft 7¾in)
HEIGHT	4.00m (13ft 1½in)
WEIGHT EMPTY	2,700kg (5,953lb)
WEIGHT LOADED	3,800kg (8,379lb)
MAX SPEED	200km/h (124mph)
SERVICE CEILING	7,000m (22,966ft)
NORMAL RANGE	700km (435 miles)

Top left: *Professor Heinrich Focke (left) with Cornelius Edzard standing in front of the F 19a.*

Far left: *The prototype A 20 Habicht before receiving the registration D–1159.*

Left: *Only one prototype of the A 21 photographic-reconnaissance aircraft was completed, the type being a development of the A 17.*

GL 22

In 1927 Focke-Wulf began development of an improved version of the GL 18 to be powered by two Siemens Sh 12 engines. Designated GL 22, the new aircraft was similar to the GL 18 but featured a square-shaped nose and deeper section fuselage. The braced undercarriage was of wider track and the twin 125hp Siemens Sh 12 seven-cylinder air-cooled radials were mounted below the wings. About three GL 22s were built, these being used for light transport and crew training duties.

Specification

POWERPLANTS	2 × 125hp Siemens Sh 12 radials
SPAN	16.00m (52ft 6in)
LENGTH	11.00m (36ft 1in)
HEIGHT	3.00m (9ft 10in)
WEIGHT EMPTY	1,180kg (2,601lb)
WEIGHT LOADED	1,820kg (4,013lb)
MAX SPEED	156km/h (97mph)
SERVICE CEILING	3,500m (11,482ft)
NORMAL RANGE	900km (559 miles)

W 4

During 1927 Heinrich Focke began development of a single-engined biplane reconnaissance and postal aircraft with twin floats. Designated Focke-Wulf W 4, the machine was a tandem two-seat cantilever biplane with no interplane struts. The fuselage was built of steel tube with fabric covering, the top decking sloping upwards at a slight angle from the rear cockpit to merge with the rudder. The braced tailplane was mounted high up on the rear of the fuselage and a large ventral fin ter-

The GL 22 was an improved development of the GL 18 twin-engined trainer and transport.

minated in a rudder which protruded well below the line of the fuselage. The wooden wing had rounded tips and was fabric covered, and twin all-metal floats were braced to the fuselage.

The Focke-Wulf W 4 made its first flight early in 1928, the machine differing from the original project by introducing a modified rudder, the top of which protruded well above the line of the rear fuselage. The aircraft was powered by an uncowled Gnome-Rhone Jupiter VI RK 5.3 nine-cylinder air-cooled radial which delivered 475hp for take-off. The few W 4s that were completed were delivered to the DVS (See) training schools late in 1928.

Specification

POWERPLANT	1 × 475hp Gnome-Rhone Jupiter radial
SPAN	12.35m (40ft 6¼in)
LENGTH	11.87m (38ft 11⅓in)
HEIGHT	4.56m (14ft 11½in)
WEIGHT EMPTY	1,700kg (3,748lb)
WEIGHT LOADED	2,985kg (6,581lb)
MAX SPEED	210km/h (130mph)
SERVICE CEILING	5,000m (16,404ft)
NORMAL RANGE	600km (373 miles)

S 24 Kiebitz

Early in 1928 Focke-Wulf designed the S 24 *Kiebitz* (Peewit) two-seat trainer and sporting aircraft. Although built in relatively small numbers the S 24 proved very successful and eventually led to the Fw 44 *Steiglitz* which later achieved world-wide fame.

The S 24 was a single-bay biplane with a fixed tailskid undercarriage. The fuselage was built of steel tube with fabric covering and accommodated a crew of two in tandem seats. The wings were constructed of wood with fabric covering, the lower surface possessing a dihedral of 3.5 degrees. Large 'N' section interplane struts were supplemented by wire bracing and the ailerons were interconnected by 'I' section struts. The machine was powered by an uncowled Siemens Sh 13 five-cylinder radial engine which produced 60hp for take-off. A feature of the design were the large auxiliary fuel tanks which could be carried on both sides of the fuselage.

First flown late in 1928, the *Kiebitz* established two important records during 1929. These were an endurance record of 994.8 miles with test pilots Edzard and Middendorf at the controls and a distance flight of 826.4 miles when piloted by Edzard and Harzog. The S 24 also became the favourite mount of Gerd Achgelis, the aerobatic ace. Apart from making a record-breaking 37-minute inverted flight, Achgelis also won the 1931 *Deutsche Kunstflugmeisterschaft* (German Aerobatic Championship) whilst flying the S 24.

The *Kiebitz* was followed by a project for a four-engined long-range transport aircraft, the Focke-Wulf G 25 *Kormoran*

The unusual Focke-Wulf W 4 cantilever biplane floatplane was delivered to the DVS for trials.

(Cormorant). Because of the financial situation prevailing in Germany at the time, the G 25 project had to be abandoned.

Specification

POWERPLANT	1 × 60hp Siemens Sh 13 radial
SPAN	8.90m (29ft 2⅓in)
LENGTH	6.25m (20ft 6in)
HEIGHT	2.25m (7ft 4½in)
WEIGHT EMPTY	350kg (772lb)
WEIGHT LOADED	670kg (1,256lb)
MAX SPEED	150km/h (93mph)
SERVICE CEILING	3,500m (11,482ft)

A 26

The Focke-Wulf A 26 was simply a re-designation of the A 17a D–1342 (w/nr 42) *Emden* modified for use by the Deutsche Versuchsanstalt für Luftfahrt e.V. at Berlin-Adlershof. The A 26 was designed mainly as an engine test bed, and is known to have been fitted with the 480hp Siemens-built Bristol Jupiter nine-cylinder radial and the 450hp BMW VI twelve-cylinder liquid-cooled in-line. Unfortunately no details of the experimental work carried out by the A 26 have survived.

Specification

POWERPLANT	1 × 480hp Siemens Jupiter radial
SPAN	20.00m (65ft 7¼in)
LENGTH	13.20m (43ft 3⅔in)
HEIGHT	4.00m (13ft 1½in)
WEIGHT EMPTY	2,323kg (5,122lb)
WEIGHT LOADED	4,000kg (8,818lb)
MAX SPEED	200km/h (124mph)
SERVICE CEILING	5,000m (16,404ft)
NORMAL RANGE	700km (435 miles)

The highly successful S 24 Kiebitz trainer, which eventually led to the Fw 44 Stieglitz.

An unusual feature of the S 24 were the large auxiliary fuel tanks which could be attached to the sides of the fuselage.

A 28 Habicht

The Focke-Wulf A 28 *Habicht* (Hawk) was a further refinement of the basic A 20 airframe. Of similar structure and appearance to the A 20a, the A 28 differed in being powered by a 220hp Gnome-Rhone Titan five-cylinder air-cooled radial engine. Construction of the A 28 began in 1929, the only aircraft to be completed making its first flight in March 1930. Registered D–1664 (w/nr 60) the aircraft was delivered to Luftverkehrsgesellschaft Wilhelmshaven-Rüstringen and later Norddeutsche Luftverkehr. In 1934 the machine was re-registered D–OXYK and finally passed to Lufthansa in 1937.

Specification

POWERPLANT	One 220hp Gnome-Rhone Titan radial
SPAN	16.00m (52ft 6in)
LENGTH	10.20m (33ft 5½in)
HEIGHT	3.00m (9ft 10in)
WEIGHT EMPTY	1,100kg (2,425lb)
WEIGHT LOADED	1,900kg (4,188lb)
MAX SPEED	180km/h (112mph)
SERVICE CEILING	4,500m (14,763ft)
NORMAL RANGE	700km (435 miles)

A 29 Möwe

The success of the Focke-Wulf A 17 *Möwe* (Seagull) led to the development of a more powerful version known as the A 29. Produced in 1929, the Focke-Wulf A 29 was basically the airframe of the A 17 powered by the 650hp BMW VI twelve-cylinder in-line engine. The new type could easily be distinguished from the A 17 by its blunt nose and car-type radiator.

As far as is known only five A 29s were completed, four of these being delivered to Lufthansa. These were D–1757 *Friesland* (w/nr 61), D–1775 *Jeverland* (w/nr 62),

The only A 28 Habicht *to be completed during its service with Luftverkehrsgesellschaft Wilhelmshaven-Rüstringen.*

D–1867 *Westfalen* (w/nr 58) and D–1922 *Saarland* (w/nr 63). These were used on DLH's Berlin–Paris, Berlin–Marienbad, Berlin–Berne and Berlin–Konigsburg routes, continuing to operate the two last named services until 1932.

The fifth aircraft to be completed, D–2178 (w/nr 114) was delivered to the German airline pilots' training school, Deutsche Verkehrsfliegerschule GmbH (DVS). Apart from the training of commercial pilots, DVS, which had bases at Berlin–Staaken, Schleissheim and Brunswick, also undertook the instruction of aviators for the clandestine military arm. After 1932, the four Lufthansa A 29s were transferred to less important services, but by 1934 they had disappeared from the airline's fleet list.

Specification

POWERPLANT	1 × 650hp BMW VI 6,0 in-line
SPAN	20.00m (65ft 7¼in)
LENGTH	14.80m (48ft 6¾in)
HEIGHT	4.00m (13ft 1½in)
WEIGHT EMPTY	2,710kg (5,974lb)
WEIGHT LOADED	4,400kg (9,700lb)
MAX SPEED	200km/h (124mph)
SERVICE CEILING	4,700m (15,419ft)
NORMAL RANGE	1,300km (808 miles)

A 32 Bussard

In 1929 Focke-Wulf began development of a six-passenger transport under the designation A 32 *Bussard* (Buzzard). The A 32 was a high-wing monoplane with a fixed undercarriage braced to the lower fuselage and the underside of the wing. The fuselage was built of steel tube with metal panels covering the nose forward of the enclosed cockpit and fabric aft. The wing was a spruce box spar structure with plywood covering, the typical Focke-Wulf Zanonia-planform being utilised. The wooden tailplane was wire braced and the fin and rudder were metal structures with fabric

Four of the five A 29s to be completed were delivered to Lufthansa. This aircraft was named Friesland.

The second A 32 Bussard in service with Nordbayerische Verkehrsflug during the early 1930s.

covering. The *Bussard* was powered by a 280/310hp Junkers L 5 inverted in-line engine driving a two-bladed airscrew.

The first two A 32s were delivered in 1930, being allocated the civil registrations D–1910 (w/nr 95) and D–1942 (w/nr 96). Both aircraft were delivered to Nordbayerische Verkehrsflug (which later became Deutsche Verkehrsflug) and used on the airline's Dresden–Nuremburg, Plauen–Berlin and Dortmund–Borkum services.

Three other A 32s were completed during 1931, two of these D–1997 (w/nr 104) and D–2129 (w/nr 113) being delivered to the Deutsche Verkehrsfliegerschule. The remaining aircraft, D–2079 (w/nr 105) was delivered to the DVL at Berlin-Adlershof. In 1934 the first two aircraft (w/nrs 95 and 96) were taken over by Deutsche Lufthansa with the new registrations D–OBES and D–ODUL respectively. The airline used the machines on their Bremen–Nuremburg service for a short time.

Specification

POWERPLANT	1 × 310hp Junkers L 5 in-line
SPAN	16.00m (52ft 6in)
LENGTH	12.20m (40ft 0in)
HEIGHT	3.25m (10ft 8in)
WEIGHT EMPTY	1,465kg (3,229lb)
WEIGHT LOADED	2,300kg (5,070lb)
MAX SPEED	190km/h (118mph)
SERVICE CEILING	4,500m (14,763ft)
NORMAL RANGE	800km (497 miles)

A 33 Sperber

The Focke-Wulf A 33 *Sperber* (Sparrowhawk) was a light airliner and taxi aircraft built early in 1930. It was a shoulder-wing monoplane powered by a single Walter Mars nine-cylinder air-cooled radial engine which developed 145hp for take-off.

The fuselage of the A 33 was a welded steel tube structure with plywood covering around the cabin and fabric aft. The pilot sat above and behind the engine, and a small cabin was provided for three passengers. The wing, which was of typical Focke-Wulf planform, was built entirely of wood. The fixed undercarriage was braced to the underside of the wing and the lower longerons and a small tailskid was provided beneath the rear fuselage.

The *Sperber* was offered for sale at an overall cost of 30,500 RM (approximately £1,500 Sterling) but, as far as is known, only three were sold. These were D–1851 (w/nr 91) bought by Norddeutsche Luftverkehr AG of Bremen, D–1931 (w/nr 97) delivered to Luftverkehrsgesellschaft Wilhelmshaven-Rüstringen and D–2153 (w/nr 115) sold to a private owner. The second aircraft, (w/nr 97), was later transferred to Lufthansa as D–ONUT.

Specification

POWERPLANT	1 × 145hp Walter Mars radial
SPAN	12.00m (39ft 4½in)
LENGTH	9.58m (31ft 5¼in)
HEIGHT	3.00m (9ft 10in)
WEIGHT EMPTY	670kg (1,477lb)
WEIGHT LOADED	1,120kg (2,469lb)
MAX SPEED	165km/h (102mph)
SERVICE CEILING	3,000m (9,842ft)
NORMAL RANGE	550km (342 miles)

The prototype A 33 Sperber *before being registered D–1851 and delivered to Norddeutsche Luftverkehr.*

A 36

Towards the end of 1929 Lufthansa requested the development of a high-speed postal aircraft capable of carrying 300kg of mail at a cruising speed of about 140mph over a distance of almost 1,000 miles. Two companies became interested in the requirement; BFW and Focke-Wulf.

Designated A 36, the Focke-Wulf project was for a bulky low-wing monoplane powered by a 525hp BMW Hornet radial engine. The wing was of typical Focke-Wulf planform, but the fuselage was a short stubby structure built of metal with fabric covering. Large 'trouser' fairings partly enclosed the mainwheels and were braced to the fuselage centre-line by diagonal struts.

Between June 20th and July 4th, 1930 a model of the A 36 was extensively tested in the AVA windtunnel at Göttingen under the designation 'Modell 2634'. Construction of a prototype began during the summer of 1931 the aircraft being delivered later in the year. The machine was similar in appearance to that originally proposed, although the 'trouser' fairings were omitted. Unfortunately no details of the A 36's subsequent career have survived, and as far as is known, no civil registration was allocated.

The BFW competitor, the Messerschmitt M 28, was delivered to Lufthansa in 1932, but was soon rendered obsolete by the Lockheed Orion with Swissair. This spurred the German aircraft industry to greater efforts, resulting in the production of the He 70 and Ju 160.

Specification

POWERPLANT	1 × 525hp BMW Hornet radial
SPAN	14.00m (45ft 11¼in)
LENGTH	10.30m (33ft 9½in)
HEIGHT	4.00m (13ft 1½in)
WEIGHT EMPTY	1,280kg (2,822lb)
WEIGHT LOADED	2,400kg (5,292lb)
MAX SPEED	260km/h (162mph)
SERVICE CEILING	5,000m (16,404ft)
NORMAL RANGE	1,600km (994 miles)

An unusual photograph of the experimental Focke-Wulf A 36 postal aircraft of which only one prototype was built.

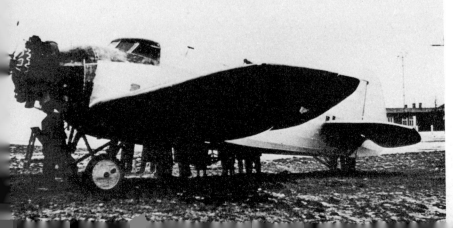

A 38 Möwe

The final version of the *Möwe* series of airliners was the Focke-Wulf A 38 built during 1931. The A 38 employed the same wing as the A 17 and A 29, but introduced a more streamlined fuselage with accommodation for pilot and co-pilot, a radio operator and ten passengers. The fuselage, like that of the previous *Möwe* types, was built of steel tube, but employed all fabric covering. A modified and considerably strengthened main undercarriage was provided, and the skid was replaced by a semi-recessed tailwheel.

Four A 38s were built during 1931, all being powered initially by the 400hp Siemens-built Bristol Jupiter nine-cylinder air-cooled radial engine. This engine was uncowled featuring a large collector ring for the exhaust gases, and drove a two-bladed wooden airscrew. At a later date the aircraft were fitted with the Siemens Sh 20u air-cooled radial which developed 500hp for take-off. The modified version was known as the A 38b.

The Focke-Wulf A 38 was the last of a series of Möwe *transports produced by the company. D-2073* Bückeburg *was delivered to Lufthansa.*

All four aircraft, D–2073 (w/nr 108) *Bückeburg*, D–2082 (w/nr 109) *Hessen*, D–2107 (w/nr 110) *Lipper* and D–2114 (w/nr 111) *Thüringen* were delivered to Lufthansa and used by the airline until 1933. A large number of services were flown by the A 38 including those between Berlin and Paris (via Leipzig), Berlin and Paris (via Cologne), Berlin and Berne, Berlin and Munich, Berlin and Vienna, Berlin and Oslo and Munich and Saarbrücken. By 1934, the aircraft had been replaced by the famous Ju 52/3m airliner.

Specification (A 38)

POWERPLANT	One 400hp Siemens Jupiter radial
SPAN	20.00m (65ft 7¼in)
LENGTH	15.40m (50ft 6¼in)
HEIGHT	5.30m (17ft 4⅔in)
WEIGHT EMPTY	2,200kg (4,850lb)
WEIGHT LOADED	4,400kg (9,700lb)
MAX SPEED	204km/h (127mph)
SERVICE CEILING	3,500m (11,482ft)
NORMAL RANGE	750km (466 miles)

A 39

Simultaneously with the design of the A 36 mailplane and the S 48 trainer/transport, Focke-Wulf began work on a two-seat reconnaissance aircraft. This machine, designated A 39, employed the modified fuselage and tail assembly of the A 36 but introduced a parasol wing to afford the crew an uninterrupted view of the ground. The wing and sturdily braced wide-track undercarriage were attached to the fuselage by a complex system of struts, and a fixed tailskid was provided. The pilot and observer were seated high up above the bulky fuselage in tandem open cockpits.

The prototype A 39 was completed during 1931, being powered by a 510hp Siemens Jupiter nine-cylinder air-cooled radial driving a fixed-pitch wooden airscrew. After extensive testing, the A 39 was delivered to the clandestine air training school at Lipezk in Russia for evaluation, but no production orders were forthcoming. Apart from the fact that the A 39 had a maximum speed of 265km/h (165mph) no specification figures are available.

A 40

When Kurt Tank took over as Technical Director of Focke-Wulf he continued the development of several designs. One of these was the A 40, a short-range reconnaissance aircraft designed to a specification issued in 1930 by the Reichswehrministerium.

The Focke-Wulf A 40 was a parasol wing monoplane with a fixed, spatted and heavily braced undercarriage. The fuselage was built of welded steel tube with fabric covering and the wing was constructed of spruce with plywood covering. Provision was made for a crew of two, pilot and observer, seated in tandem open cockpits. The aircraft was powered by a Siemens SAM 22B nine-cylinder air-cooled radial engine which produced 660hp for take-off.

As far as is known, only one prototype of the A 40 was completed, this later being redesignated as the Fw 40 under the new RLM designation system. In many ways ahead of its time, the Fw 40 proved very unstable and despite intensive work, Tank failed to cure this trouble. The type was designed to compete with the He 46, but its flight characteristics were such that the outcome of the contest was a foregone conclusion, the Heinkel design easily emerging as victor. No specification figures are available for the A 40.

Left: With its bulky fuselage and large radial engine, the Focke-Wulf A 39 bore considerable similarity to the A 36 and S 48.

27

W 7

In 1931 the Reichswehrministerium requested the development of a light bomber and long-range reconnaissance aircraft from the Heinkel and Focke-Wulf companies. For some obscure reason the Focke-Wulf project was designated W 7. It was a sturdy single-bay biplane with twin open cockpits and a fixed undercarriage. The fuselage was built of welded steel tube with fabric covering and the wing was constructed of spruce with plywood covering. The upper wing was braced to the fuselage by four single struts and large N-section interplane struts were provided. The fixed undercarriage was also designed to be replaced by twin floats.

The W 7 made its first flight in 1932 powered by a 660hp BMW VI 6,0 twelve-cylinder liquid-cooled in-line engine driving a four-bladed wooden airscrew. The W 7 was delivered, like the A 39, to the Lipezk training school in Russia for evaluation, but the competing Heinkel design, the He 45, proved far superior and the Focke-Wulf machine was abandoned. Apart from the fact that a maximum speed of 250km/h (155mph) was attained, no specification figures are available for the W 7.

Top left: *Only one prototype of the A 40 short-range reconnaissance aircraft was produced. Despite several advanced features, it failed to reach the production stage.*

Bottom left: *Only one Focke-Wulf W 7 was completed, the aircraft undergoing trials at the Lipezk training school in the USSR.*

A 43 Falke

The Focke-Wulf A 43 *Falke* (Falcon) was the last aircraft designed by Heinrich Focke before he left the company to concentrate on rotorcraft development. Produced early in 1932, the *Falke* was a high-speed transport and communications aircraft powered by a 220hp Argus As 10 eight-cylinder air-cooled in-line engine.

A conventional high-wing monoplane, the A 43 carried a pilot and two passengers seated in tandem inside an enclosed cabin. The fuselage, tailfin and rudder were constructed of welded steel tube with fabric covering. The wing was of familiar Zanonia-form construction, built of spruce with plywood covering between the two box spars. The remainder of the wing and the wooden tailplane were covered with fabric. The wing was braced to the fuselage by V struts and the divided undercarriage was fitted with large spats.

The highly polished A 43, D–2333 (w/nr 127) made its first flight during the early summer of 1932 with Focke's test pilot Cornelius Edzard at the controls. The machine was delivered to Norddeutsche Luftverkehr in August 1932, who claimed it to be the fastest transport aircraft in Europe at that time. Despite its exceptional performance, only one A 43 (later designated Fw under the new RLM designation system) was built.

Specification

POWERPLANT	1 × 220hp Argus As 10 in-line
SPAN	10.00m (32ft 9½in)
LENGTH	8.30m (27ft 2¾in)
HEIGHT	2.30m (7ft 6½in)
WEIGHT EMPTY	725kg (1,598lb)
WEIGHT LOADED	1,125kg (2,480lb)
MAX SPEED	255km/h (158mph)
SERVICE CEILING	5,100m (16,732ft)
NORMAL RANGE	1,050km (652 miles)

When delivered in 1932, the A 43 Falke *was claimed to be the fastest transport aircraft in Europe.*

Fw 44 Stieglitz

Until the production of the Fw 44 during the early 1930s, the name of Focke-Wulf was virtually unknown outside Germany, and then it was frequently confused with the Dutch Fokker company. Apart from being built in larger numbers than any other Focke type except for the Fw 190, the Fw 44 was sold to many foreign owners, and also built under licence in Austria, Argentina, Brazil, Bulgaria and Sweden.

Design work on the A 44 (as the type was originally designated) was completed early in 1932, it being a single bay biplane trainer and sporting aircraft with two tandem seats. The wings, which had slight dihedral and sweepback, were constructed of a mixture of pine and plywood with part plywood and part fabric covering. The fuselage was constructed of welded steel tube with fabric covering apart from a small section around the nose which was metal. The upper wing was supported above the fuselage by N-section struts and inverted N-section interplane struts were provided. Each mainwheel was mounted on a large streamlined leg which was braced to the lower fuselage.

During the late summer of 1932, the prototype, the Focke-Wulf A 44a (D–2409) made its first flight with Gerd Achgelis at the controls. The aircraft was powered by a 140hp Siemens Sh 14a seven-cylinder air-cooled radial driving a two-bladed wooden airscrew. Two fuel tanks with a total capacity of 135 litres (29.7 Imp gals) were mounted in the fuselage forward of a fireproof bulkhead. Aft of this bulkhead were the two tandem seats, the rear of which could be folded for access to a small parcel space. Full dual controls were provided, the instructor sitting in the rear seat.

The prototype A 44, which was named *Stieglitz* (Goldfinch) in Focke-Wulf's series of bird names, displayed several unfortunate flying characteristics. After Kurt Tank joined the company he took over flight testing of the aircraft, and following a considerable number of minor modifications, the flight characteristics were immensely improved.

After the new RLM aircraft designation system was introduced early in 1933, the Focke-Wulf A 44 became the Fw 44. The second prototype, the Fw 44b differed in being powered by a 135hp Argus As 8 four-cylinder in-line engine in a considerably lengthened cowling. During 1933 the Fw 44 competed with the somewhat similar Arado Ar 69 for a contract to provide the still secret Luftwaffe with a primary trainer. The excellent performance now displayed by the *Stieglitz* made the result of the competition a foregone conclusion.

Three further prototypes were constructed with the Siemens Sh 14a radial, designated Fw 44c, d and f. The latter was fitted with full operational equipment and was delivered to the Luftwaffe as the Fw

Top right: *The prototype Focke-Wulf Fw 44a (D–2409) powered by a 140hp Siemens Sh 14 radial.*

Bottom right: *A number of Fw 44Es were completed, the variant differing in being powered by an Argus As 8 in-line engine.*

30

44F production series. A second Argus As 8 powered prototype was also built under the designation Fw 44e, a small number of production aircraft being delivered as the Fw 44E.

The *Stieglitz* formed the initial equipment of many early Luftwaffe units including the *Fliegergruppen* at Göppingen, Neuhausen, Schleissheim, Merseburg, Delmenhorst, Ansbach, Erfurt and Nordhausen. These units were later redesignated Aufkl.Gr 15 and 121, I./JG 334, I./KG 153, III./KG 154, II./KG 155 and II. and III./KG 253 respectively. The *Stieglitz* was also used by the *Fliegerschulen* at Magdeburg, Oldenburg and Stettin, the DVS at Berlin, Würzburg and Schleissheim and various sections of the Deutsche Luftsportverband.

Apart from the military and paramilitary organisations, the Fw 44 was also delivered to many private owners. Included amongst these were the aerobatic experts Ernst Udet, Gerd Achgelis and Emil Kropf. During the middle 1930s Achgelis made a tour of America with the Fw 44 which did much to impress potential foreign buyers. During the period that preceded World War II the *Stieglitz* was delivered to Bolivia, Chile, China, Czechoslovakia, Finland, Rumania, Switzerland,

Top left: *An early production Fw 44F (D–2692) which was named* Hptm Boelcke *after the famous fighter pilot of World War I.*

Bottom left: *A late production Fw 44F (D–EUKA) which was delivered in large numbers to the Luftwaffe's trainer elements.*

31

This Focke-Wulf Fw 44J carries the post-war civil registration D–EBOB.

Turkey, Austria, Argentina, Bulgaria, Brazil and Sweden, the last five countries producing the machine under licence.

Just before the war, an improved version of the *Stieglitz* was built under the designation Fw 44J. Powered by a more powerful Siemens Sh 14A engine which developed 150hp for take-off, the variant saw widespread service with the Luftwaffe's training schools. These included FFS A/B 4 at Prague, A/B 43 at Crailsheim, A/B 51 at Elbing, A/B 72 at Markersdorf, A/B 112 at Langenlebarn, A/B 113 at Brünn, A/B 125 at Neukuhren and FFS C 22 at Oels. Several of these aircraft were fitted with skis for winter operations.

After the war, many Fw 44s remained in service with various air arms and private owners. The last aircraft did not disappear from service in Sweden and Switzerland until the latter part of the 1950s.

Specification (Fw 44F)

POWERPLANT	1 × 140hp Siemens Sh 14a radial
SPAN	9.00m (29ft 6½in)
LENGTH	7.30m (23ft 11½in)
HEIGHT	2.70m (8ft 10¼in)
WEIGHT EMPTY	560kg (1,235lb)
WEIGHT LOADED	900kg (1,985lb)
MAX SPEED	188km/h (117mph)
SERVICE CEILING	4,400m (14,435ft)
NORMAL RANGE	540km (335 miles)

(Fw 44E)
Figures similar to the above with the following exceptions:

POWERPLANT	1 × 135hp Argus As 8 in-line
LENGTH	7.70m (25ft 3in)
MAX SPEED	185km/h (115mph)
SERVICE CEILING	3,900m (12,795ft)
NORMAL RANGE	600km (373 miles)

Fw 47

In December 1930 Prof Kurt Wegener of the German meteorological service asked Focke-Wulf to develop a specialised weather reconnaissance aircraft. Design work on the new type, the Focke-Wulf A 47, was completed in September 1931, a mock-up being inspected by the *Zentrale für Flugsicherung* (Centre for Air Safety) and the *Wetterflugstelle* (Air Weather Station) at Hamburg.

The prototype, later registered D–2295, made its first flight in June 1932 with Cornelius Edzard at the controls. The A 47 was a tandem two-seat parasol wing monoplane with a fixed undercarriage. The fuselage was constructed of steel tube with fabric covering and the wing, of typical Zanonia-form, was built of wood throughout. The aircraft was powered by a single 195/220hp Argus As 10 eight-cylinder air-cooled in-line engine driving a two-bladed wooden airscrew.

After extensive tests by the *Reichsverband der Deutschen Luftfahrtindustrie* (Federation of German aviation industries) at Travemünde, the A 47 was delivered to the Hamburg weather station in December 1932 for operational trials. During 1934 and 1935 at least nine of the first production model (designated Fw 47C) were delivered. These included D–IGYH, D–INYP, D–IPIN and D–IREZ delivered in September 1934, D–IVYL and D–IVYM in October, D–IZAK in May 1935 and D–IBVY in November.

The Fw 47C differed from the prototype in being powered by a 240hp Argus As 10C engine, having a modified rear cockpit with a windscreen for the observer and the

addition of radio equipment. The Fw 47D (of which at least 11 aircraft were completed) was similar, but was powered by the Argus As 10E engine with improved high altitude capabilities. Deliveries of the Fw 47D were made between January and April 1936 and included D–IGBU, D–IJTE, D–ILBA, D–IOLY, D–IPRA, D–ISFA, D–ITLO, D–ITPO, D–IUNE and D–IXLU. Perhaps the most interesting of these aircraft was the latter, D–IXLU which, delivered to the Königsberg weather station in 1936, was fitted with a ski undercarriage.

The Fw 47 was delivered to weather research stations all over Germany, performing much useful work for many years. Even at the end of the war one aircraft was recorded as being held in reserve by the Schleissheim weather station near Munich.

Specification (Fw 47C)

POWERPLANT	1 × 240hp Argus As 10C in-line
SPAN	17.76m (58ft 3in)
LENGTH	10.57m (34ft 8in)
HEIGHT	3.04m (9ft 11¾in)
WEIGHT EMPTY	1,065kg (2,348lb)
WEIGHT LOADED	1,580kg (3,484lb)
MAX SPEED	190km/h (118mph)
SERVICE CEILING	5,600m (18,372ft)
NORMAL RANGE	640km (398 miles)

Top left: *The prototype Fw 47 meteorological reconnaissance aircraft which was delivered to the Hamburg weather station in 1932.*

Bottom left: *The Fw 47C differed in being powered by an Argus As 10C engine. This machine (D–IVYL) was delivered in October 1934.*

S 48

The Focke-Wulf S 48 was a project for a tandem two-seat trainer or three-seat light transport aircraft based on the A 36 mailplane. It was a cantilever low-wing monoplane with unbraced 'trouser' fairings partly enclosing both mainwheels. The trainer variant was to have twin open cockpits positioned above the wing; the transport development having the second cockpit replaced by a small enclosed cabin for two passengers.

Consideration was given to the installation of a 200hp Siemens radial or a 200hp Argus in-line engine in the project, but the design was finalised around a 420hp Pratt & Whitney R–1430–C Wasp radial. Two wing designs were considered for the project, one with conventional rounded tips, the other of typical Focke-Wulf planform. Little interest appears to have been shown in the project, and the S 48 was abandoned in 1931 no production being undertaken.

Specification (Manufacturer's estimates)

POWERPLANT	1 × 420hp Pratt & Whitney R–1430–C Wasp radial
SPAN	13.00m (42ft 7¾in)
LENGTH	9.80m (32ft 3in)
HEIGHT	3.40m (11ft 1¾in)
MAX SPEED	240km/h (149mph)

Top right: The Focke-Wulf Fw 55 was merely a development of the Albatros L 102 with considerable structural strengthening.

Bottom right: The floatplane version of the Fw 55 introduced a small lower wing and additional fin and rudder area.

Fw 55

When Focke-Wulf absorbed the Albatros Flugzeugwerke GmbH in September 1931 it took over several designs, one of which was the L 102 trainer and sporting aircraft. Two versions of the two-seat parasol wing machine were built, the Albatros L 102L landplane and the L 102W floatplane, both powered by a 240hp Argus As 10C eight-cylinder air-cooled in-line engine.

The wings and tailplane of both aircraft were built of spruce with plywood covering and the fuselage and tailfin were mixed wood and steel tube structures with fabric covering. The wing of the landplane was supported above the fuselage by two sets of pylon-like struts and braced by V-struts. The tailplane and fixed undercarriage were also braced to the fuselage. Apart from the twin floats, the L 102W also differed in having a small lower wing and additional

auxiliary fin and rudder surfaces which extended below the line of the fuselage.

Shortly after taking over the Albatros company, Kurt Tank survived without injury a serious crash in a L 102 when demonstrating the aircraft's diving capabilities before officials of the DVS. The cause of the accident was later attributed to violent aileron oscillation which distorted the starboard wing. Therefore Tank undertook a redesign of the aircraft under the designation Fw 55.

Apart from the N-section struts which supported the wing above the fuselage, the Focke-Wulf Fw 55 was essentially similar to the Albatros L 102 (later designated A1 102) apart from some structural strengthening. A small production batch of both the Fw 55L landplane and the Fw 55W floatplane were completed, being delivered mainly to the DVS.

Specification (Fw 55L)

POWERPLANT	1 × 240hp Argus As 10C in-line
SPAN	13.40m (43ft 9½in)
LENGTH	9.07m (29ft 9in)
HEIGHT	2.66m (8ft 8⅔in)
WEIGHT EMPTY	795kg (1,653lb)
WEIGHT LOADED	1,230kg (2,712lb)
MAX SPEED	217km/h (135mph)
SERVICE CEILING	5,400m (17,716ft)

Right: For some reason the prototype Fw 56 was incorrectly registered D–JSOT.

Fw 56 Stösser

During the early 1930s, the RLM placed a specification for a lightweight fighter and advanced trainer to be powered by a 240hp Argus As 10C in-line engine. Three companies produced designs; Arado the Ar 76, Heinkel the He 74 and Focke-Wulf the Fw 56 *Stösser* (Hawk).

The Fw 56 was designed by *Dipl Ing* Kurt Tank in 1932, its general outlines obviously owing something to previous aircraft produced by the Albatros company. The parasol wing was built of spruce and plywood with stressed plywood covering forward of the rear spar and fabric aft. The fuselage was constructed of welded steel tube with part alloy and part fabric covering. The wing was attached to the fuselage forward of the single open cockpit by N-struts, and braced by V-struts to the lower fuselage longerons. The mainwheels were neatly spatted and a tailskid was provided beneath the rear fuselage. The tail assembly was of typical Albatros design with a braced horizontal stabiliser.

The prototype *Stösser* (incorrectly marked D–JSOT instead of D–ISOT) made its first flight in November 1933, with the designation Fw 56a. Early tests showed that the shock absorption characteristics of the undercarriage were not very satisfactory and that the faired headrest impaired the view to the rear. Therefore, the second aircraft, the Fw 56b D–IIKA, had the headrest removed and new, much broader undercarriage legs fitted. The machine also differed in having a wing of all-metal construction, and a vane-operated controllable pitch airscrew of Argus design was later fitted.

After initial tests with the second *Stösser* prototype, it was realised that its undercarriage was very similar to that patented by the French Messier company, with the consequence that it was again quickly redesigned. The Fw 56 V3 (the Fw 56a and b having been renamed VI and V2 respectively under the new RLM designation system adopted in 1934) first flew in February 1934. It differed from the V2 in having new narrower chord under-

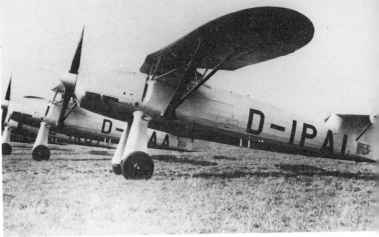

The Fw 56 V4 (otherwise known as the A–01) was the first of a batch of three pre-production aircraft.

A line-up of five Fw 56A–1 production aircraft prior to being delivered to the Luftwaffe.

carriage legs, unspatted wheels and a wing of similar construction to the first aircraft.

A competition was held at Rechlin during the summer of 1935 to make a final decision on the merits of the three designs. Eventually the Fw 56 was adjudged superior mainly on account of its structural strength, the RLM placing the Ar 76 second and completely abandoning the He 74. The Ar 76 was somewhat similar to the Fw 56 in appearance, but the He 74 biplane* although fast and manoeuvrable, was considered somewhat outmoded.

Meanwhile a batch of three Fw 56A–0 pre-production aircraft had been ordered, all of which were given an alternative *Versuchs* (experimental) number. The Fw 56A–01 (alias V4) registered D–ITAU,

* See *Heinkel—An Aircraft Album*, page 73.

was fitted with armament and introduced several minor modifications to the engine cowling and wing structure. The machine was also fitted with a small dive brake aft of the leading edge of the wing centre-section which allowed it to attain over 300mph in a dive.

The Fw 56 V4 carried two 7.9mm MG 17 machine-guns in the upper fuselage decking and a small internal bay was provided for three 22lb SD 10 bombs. Tests were also made with MG 34 sub machine-guns fixed to the V-struts, but these proved unsuccessful and were abandoned. The Fw 56A–02 (V5) D–IGEU was similar to the fourth aircraft but the A–03 (V6) D–IXYO carried only one MG 17 weapon.

Early in 1936, the *Inspekteur der Jagd und Stukaflieger, Oberst* Ernst Udet, test flew the Fw 56 V2 at Berlin-Johannisthal.

He was so impressed by the exceptional diving performance of the aircraft that he asked for it to be fitted with practice bombs. Apart from the controllable-pitch airscrew mentioned earlier, the Fw 56 V2 was fitted with two racks beneath the wings, each of which could carry three 2.2 lb NB 1 smoke bombs. It was found that when the Fw 56 released its bombs in a dive it achieved a much higher standard of accuracy than in level flight. The trials, conducted by *Flugkapitän* Wolfgang Stein, helped to advance the theories of Ernst Udet regarding the dive bomber.

The success of the *Stösser* led to a contract being placed for the Fw 56A–1 production model. This variant was generally similar to the three Fw 56A–0s, being powered by the 240hp Argus As 10C eight-cylinder air-cooled in-line engine.

A standard production Fw 56A–1 in service with a Luftwaffe fighter-training school.

Provision was made for one or two 7.9mm MG 17 machine-guns above the engine cowling, but these were not always fitted.

Apart from extensive deliveries to the Luftwaffe, the Fw 56 was also used by the NSFK and exported to Austria and Hungary. In the Luftwaffe the *Stösser* served mainly as an advanced trainer with the *Jagd* and *Stuka Fliegerschulen* (Fighter and Dive Bomber Pilot Schools) although the type is known to have been used by the initial training units FFS A/B 41 at Frankfurt am Oder and FFS A/B 112 at Langenlebarn/Tulln.

A few Fw 56A–1s were delivered to private pilots, the most famous of which was undoubtedly D–IKNI flown by the aerobatic expert Gerd Achgelis. Other *Stössers* were delivered to DFS for experiments as a pick-a-back aircraft to carry the

DFS 230 glider, and one machine was fitted with a 660lb thrust Walter rocket engine. Six aircraft were delivered to IV. (Erg)/KG 200 for special test purposes. The Fw 56 was also projected with the more powerful Argus As 10K, As 410 and As 417 engines, but no production was undertaken.

Specification (Fw 56A–1)

POWERPLANT	1 × 240hp Argus As 10C in-line
SPAN	10.50m (34ft 5½in)
LENGTH	7.60m (24ft 11¼ in)
HEIGHT	2.60m (8ft 6⅓in)
WEIGHT EMPTY	755kg (1,665lb)
WEIGHT LOADED	985kg (2,172lb)
MAX SPEED	278km/h (173mph)
SERVICE CEILING	6,200m (20,341ft)
NORMAL RANGE	385km (239 miles)

Fw 57

The Fw 57 was Focke-Wulf's first venture into the field of all-metal stressed-skin construction. It was conceived in answer to an RLM specification issued during the late autumn of 1934 which called for a long-range heavy fighter or *Kampfzerstörer*. The specification was issued to six companies; AGO, BFW, Dornier, Focke-Wulf, Gotha, Heinkel and Henschel. After an initial examination in December 1934, three of these projects were chosen for further evaluation, the BFW Bf 110, the Henschel Hs 124 and the Focke-Wulf Fw 57.

The largest of the three projects, the Fw 57 was designed by *Dipl Ing* Bansemir. It was a low-wing monoplane with a fully retractable tailwheel undercarriage and provision for a crew of three; pilot, bomb-aimer and gunner. The cantilever wing was built in three sections with main and auxiliary spars. The fuselage was a circular monocoque structure with a fully glazed nose section and a stepped cockpit. An electrically operated Mauser dorsal turret was developed for the project, this being designed to carry a 20mm MG FF cannon. Two further MG FF cannon were to be mounted in the nose, operated by the bomb-aimer.

Two powerplants were specified for the *Kampfzerstörer* projects, the Junkers Jumo 210 and the Daimler Benz DB 600, both twelve-cylinder liquid cooled in-lines. The Fw 57 employed two of the latter engines, each of which developed 910hp for take-off, and drove three-bladed variable-pitch metal airscrews.

The first prototype, the Fw 57 V1 made

its initial flight in the late spring of 1936 with *Flugkapitän* Wolfgang Stein at the controls. No armament was installed in the aircraft, although it did carry a mock-up of the Mauser gun turret. Trials showed that the Fw 57 V1 was seriously overweight the wing structure alone weighing some five times the figure originally calculated!

At this stage, the RLM favoured the Henschel Hs 124 of the three designs under consideration, but following the intervention of Ernst Udet, who considered the faster and lighter Bf 110 a much more promising proposition, a complete revision of the *Kampfzerstörer* specification was undertaken. The whole idea of a composite heavy fighter and light bomber was abandoned in favour of two separate aircraft; that of a *Zerstörer* or heavy fighter to which the Bf 110 was adapted, and that of a *Schnellbomber* or fast bomber to which the Ju 88 was eventually produced.

By this time the testing of the Fw 57 was purely academic. Apart from excessive structural weight, the Fw 57 also proved

to have poor handling characteristics. Eventually the Fw 57 V1 was forced to make an emergency landing in soft ground and was written off. Two further prototypes, the Fw 57 V2 and V3 were completed and flown during the summer and autumn of 1936, but by then it was realised that the aircraft was a complete failure and it was abandoned. The two later prototypes differed from the first aircraft in having a taller rudder and revised control tabs for the rudder and elevators. Like the Fw 57, both aircraft were unarmed.

Specification (Fw 57 V1)

POWERPLANTS	2 × 910hp DB 600 in-lines
SPAN	25.00m (82ft 0¼in)
LENGTH	16.40m (53ft 9⅔in)
HEIGHT	4.10m (13ft 5⅛in)
WEIGHT EMPTY	6,800kg (14,994lb)
WEIGHT LOADED	8,300kg (18,302lb)
MAX SPEED	400km/h (249mph)
SERVICE CEILING	9,100m (29,855ft)

The Fw 57 V1 bomber destroyer which failed because of its high structural weight.

Fw 58 Weihe

One of the most important crew trainers and general purpose aircraft produced for the Luftwaffe was the Fw 58 *Weihe* (Kite). A type roughly comparable with the RAF's Avro Anson, the *Weihe* was designed by *Dipl Ing* Kurt Tank and was the first Focke-Wulf aircraft to have a retractable undercarriage. It was the Fw 58 that finally solved the financial problems of the company, orders for the aircraft being received from the Luftwaffe, Lufthansa and several foreign countries.

The prototype Fw 58 V1 (D-ABEM) made its first flight during the summer of 1935. It was designed to the same requirement as the generally similar but more angular Arado Ar 77, but proved much more successful. The *Weihe* was a cantilever low-wing monoplane powered by two 240hp Argus As 10C eight-cylinder air-cooled engines. The smoothly rounded fuselage was built of steel tube with a mixture of light metal, wood and fabric covering. Provision was made for a crew of two and six passengers, access to the cabin being gained via a door in the port side of the fuselage aft of the wing.

The wing was built in three sections, comprising a rectangular centre section braced to the fuselage by single struts and two outer panels with tapered leading edges. The wing, the outer panels of which had considerable dihedral, was constructed of metal with duralumin covering forward of the mainspar and fabric aft. The mainwheels retracted into the underslung engine nacelles, and the machine had a fixed tailwheel. The braced tailplane was forward of the fin and fabric covered rudder.

A feature of the *Weihe* was the provision for rapid interchange of the nose sections for different rôles. The Fw 58 V1 had a smoothly streamlined nose, but the second aircraft, the Fw 58 V2, was a military version with provision for a 7.9mm MG 15 machine-gun in an open nose position and a similar weapon in a dorsal opening. The first three aircraft were forerunners of the proposed Fw 58A production model, but this was abandoned in favour of the Fw 58B.

The Fw 58 V4 (possibly D–APAN) was prototype for the Fw 58B, an aerodynamically refined variant which had a glazed nose with provision for a single 7.9mm MG 15 gun. A second weapon could be carried in an open dorsal position. Two production variants were built, the first being the Fw 58B–1 with a conventional nose intended for use by the Luftwaffe in the communications, training and air ambulance rôles. The Fw 58B–2 had the nose of the V4 and was intended for gunnery training. A seaplane version of the *Weihe* was also built with twin floats under the designation Fw 58BW.

In 1938, Focke-Wulf introduced the improved Fw 58C production model intended for both military and civilian use. Unlike the previous models, the Fw 58C was designed to be powered by two 240hp Argus As 10C eight-cylinder engines or two 260hp Hirth HM 508D units of similar configuration. Prototype for the C-series *Weihe* was the Fw 58 V11 powered by As 10C engines.

Eight aircraft were delivered to Lufthansa during 1938/9. Four of these, the Fw 58 V13 *Rhein* (w/nr 3100), the V14 D–OHLM *Donau* (w/nr 3101) and two

Below: *The first military prototype of the Focke-Wulf* Weihe *was fitted with twin open gun positions.*

Bottom: *A plan view of the military Fw 58 showing the aircraft's attractive lines.*

A Focke-Wulf Fw 58C communications aircraft, possibly the personal aircraft of Kurt Tank, registered D–ALEX.

One of a small batch of Fw 58BW twin floatplanes alights on the water.

Fw 58Cs D–OKDN (w/nr 3103) and D–OXVF *Elbe* (w/nr 3104) were powered by HM 508D engines. The other machines, the Fw 58 V15 D–ONBR (w/nr 2697), the V16 D–OAFD (w/nr 2698), the V17 D–OORK (w/nr 2699) and the V18 D–OBJH (w/nr 2700) were all powered by As 10C units.

One of the early *Weihe* prototypes, D–ALEX, was transferred to Kurt Tank for the designer's personal use. On one occasion Tank managed to land 'Alex', as the machine was affectionately known, without lowering the undercarriage, attributing his mistake to "a fault in the pilot's brain". Just before and during the first half of the war, Tank flew his personal *Weihe* to Moscow and North Africa. During the late spring of 1942 he journeyed to Paris, returning to Bremen via Holland. It was during this trip that he was attacked by two Spitfires. Although the aircraft was struck by 57 bullets, Tank managed to land it safely at Hilversum. After this exploit, Tank was forbidden to fly in the Fw 58, although a trip was made later to Tronheim in Norway. D–ALEX was finally destroyed on the ground by an Allied bombing attack on Paris.

As has been described, considerable use was made of the Fw 58 within the Luftwaffe. The machine served with several of the FFS A/B pilot training schools and was delivered to the staff flights of many operational *Geschwader*. The *Weihe* was also widely used for casualty evacuation, the type becoming affectionately known as the *Leukoplastbomber* by German troops. *Leukoplast* was a type of self adhesive bandage widely used in Germany.

Apart from serving widely in Germany, the Fw 58 was also delivered to Argentina, Bulgaria, China, The Netherlands, Hungary, Rumania and Sweden. Twenty-five Fw 58B–2s were built under licence by the *Fabrica do Galleao* company of Brazil, and one machine, OY–DYS (w/nr 3105) was used for a short period by the Danish airline DDL on their Copenhagen-Rønne service.

Several advanced versions of the *Weihe* were proposed, powered by the Argus As 10K, As 410 and As 417 engines, but none were built. One Fw 58C (D–OXLR) was experimentally fitted with a fixed nosewheel undercarriage for in-flight re-fuelling trials in connection with a Ju 90 tanker. An advanced replacement for the Fw 58, the Fw 206, is described in the project section.

Specification (Fw 58C)

POWERPLANTS	2 × 240hp Argus As 10C in-lines
SPAN	21.00m (68ft 10¾in)
LENGTH	14.00m (45ft 11¼in)
HEIGHT	3.90m (12ft 9½in)
WEIGHT EMPTY	2,400kg (5,291lb)
WEIGHT LOADED	3,600kg (7,936lb)
MAX SPEED	273km/h (170mph)
SERVICE CEILING	5,600m (18,372ft)
NORMAL RANGE	800km (497 miles)

Fw 62

During the summer of 1936 the RLM issued a specification for a two-seat shipboard floatplane to replace both the He 60 and the new He 114 which had already proved to have an unsatisfactory performance. Four companies were asked to submit proposals, Dornier, Gotha, Focke-Wulf and Arado. Dornier showed little interest in the specification, Gotha produced a floatplane development of their P 14 twin-engined fighter under the designation P 14–012, and the other two companies produced respectively the Fw 62 and the Ar 196.

At an early stage it was realised that the Ar 196, a low-wing monoplane with an enclosed cockpit, was much more promising than the conservative Fw 62 biplane, but nevertheless two prototypes of the latter were ordered as a back up to the Arado programme.

The Fw 62 was a conventional biplane with twin open cockpits, powered by a single 880hp BMW 132Dc nine-cylinder radial engine. The fuselage was built of welded steel tube with part metal and part fabric covering, and the equal span wings were constructed of metal with duralumin skin. Two sets of N-section interplane struts supported the top wing which was braced to the fuselage by splayed struts of similar section. The twin all-metal floats were attached to the fuselage by a specially sprung series of struts intended to cushion landing impact. An armament of one 7.9mm MG 15 machine-gun was to be

A Fw 58C communications aircraft in the rarely seen wartime markings of the Bulgarian Air Force.

The Fw 62 V1 (D–OFWF) was fitted with twin floats.

The German Air Ministry asked that the Fw 62 should have provision for either single or twin floats. Therefore the second aircraft (D–OHGF) was fitted with a single main float with two outriggers.

provided in the rear of the second cockpit on a flexible mounting.

Although produced under the overall control of Kurt Tank, the rather outdated Fw 62 was not very close to his heart, and the task of producing detailed drawings for the machine was passed to *Ing* Arbeitlang. The first prototype, the Fw 62 V1 (D–OFWF), made its initial flight in the late spring of 1937, being equipped as described with twin floats.

A requirement of the original RLM specification was that the design should be capable of being fitted with both single and twin floats. Therefore, the Fw 62 V2 (D–OHGF), which flew soon after the first aircraft, was fitted with a single main float. This was balanced by two outrigger floats braced to the wings level with the outboard interplane struts. Both prototypes were fitted with catapult spools to allow them to be launched from battleships and heavy cruisers of the Kriegsmarine.

Both prototypes were delivered to the Travemünde experimental station for extensive catapult and sea trials during the summer of 1937, and proved very satisfactory. However, despite this success, the Fw 62 was, as anticipated, abandoned in favour of the Ar 196 which was some 20mph (32km/h) faster and had the advantage of an enclosed cockpit.

Specification (Fw 62 V1)

POWERPLANT	1 × 880hp BMW 132Dc radial
SPAN	12.35m (40ft 6¼in)
LENGTH	11.15m (36ft 7in)
HEIGHT	4.30m (14ft 1¼in)
WEIGHT EMPTY	2,300kg (5,071lb)
WEIGHT LOADED	2,850kg (6,284lb)
MAX SPEED	280km/h (174mph)
SERVICE CEILING	5,900m (19,357ft)

Fw 159

Towards the mid 1930s it was being realised in the advanced aviation-minded countries that the biplane could no longer provide the increase in performance that was being demanded for new single-seat fighters. Emphasis began more and more to be placed on the monoplane; Britain producing the F.7/30 specification to which the Vickers Jockey, Bristol 133 and Supermarine 224 were designed. In France, Dewoitine built the D 510 whilst the Russian Polikarpov company produced the advanced I-16 *Rata*, both of low-wing concept. Two low-wing designs were built by Boeing of America, the P–26 and the XF7B–1, whilst Curtiss and Dayton-Wright produced respectively the XF13C–1 and XPS–1 parasol-wing monoplanes with retractable undercarriage. The parasol wing was also favoured in Poland, whilst the Dutch Fokker company built the D XXI low-wing design with a fixed undercarriage.

In 1934, the German Aviation Ministry also became interested in the design of a single-seat fighter monoplane when it issued a specification for such an aircraft to be powered by the new Junkers Jumo 210 twelve-cylinder in-line engine. Four companies submitted proposals, all, apart from that of Focke-Wulf, favouring the low-wing concept.

The Focke-Wulf aircraft was designed by *Ober Ing* R. Blaser under the supervision of *Dipl Ing* Tank and was in fact a scaled-up version of the Fw 56 *Stösser* fitted with a retractable undercarriage. It was the last named feature that made the Fw 159 such an interesting design. The mainwheel legs were double-jointed and,

The Fw 159 V2 in flight.

In this view of the Fw 159 V3, the controversial retractable undercarriage is clearly visible.

when retracted, were compressed and raised vertically into an aperture only fractionally larger than the wheel. Small doors enclosed the wheels when retracted and a tailwheel was positioned beneath the rear fuselage.

The fuselage was an oval monocoque structure built of duralumin with stressed metal skinning. Similar materials were used in the construction of the wing which was of modified NACA section. It was mounted above the centre fuselage by N-section struts and braced to the lower part of the fuselage by single streamlined struts. The enclosed cockpit was positioned just behind the wing with a rearwards sliding hood.

Extensive tests were carried out with the undercarriage retraction mechanism of the unmarked first prototype, the Fw 159 V1, before the commencement of flight trials. During these tests and previous experiments carried out with a working model,

the complicated undercarriage functioned perfectly, but not so during the aircraft's maiden flight.

The Fw 159 V1 first flew in the early summer of 1935 with the nerveless *Flugkapitän* Wolfgang Stein at the controls. The undercarriage retracted successfully, but failed to fully re-extend after thirty minutes flying. Stein was immediately assailed by a series of helpful messages painted on the ground with whitewash, and eventually another pilot took off in a Fw 56 to signal to him directly. After exhausting all his fuel, Stein attempted to land the machine, but the undercarriage collapsed and it completed two somersaults before finishing on its back. As the unhurt Stein clambered out he said, "Next time you needn't make all those damn stupid signals. If you'd left me alone I would have made a belly landing and we shouldn't have done those somersaults".

Soon after the destruction of the first

aircraft, the Fw 159 V2 (D–INGA) was completed. This introduced a strengthened undercarriage mechanism, but retained the 610hp Jumo 210A engine of the first prototype. The V3 (D–IUPY) was similar, but was powered by a 640hp Jumo 210B engine driving a two-bladed wooden airscrew. Two 7.9mm MG 17 machine-guns were mounted above the engine, and provision was made for a 20mm MG FF cannon to fire through the spinner.

During the spring of 1936, the four competing designs were evaluated at Travemünde. Neither the Arado Ar 80 (which had a fixed undercarriage) or the Fw 159 (with its unusual layout and unreliable undercarriage) were favoured, but it was not until much later that the Bf 109* was eventually considered superior to the Heinkel He 112.

Despite the rejection of the Fw 159, the

* See *Messerschmitt—An Aircraft Album*, page 39.

third aircraft was re-engined with a 730hp Jumo 210G during the summer of 1937 with which it attained a speed of 252mph. The test programme continued until 1938, during which both the Fw 159s suffered continual undercarriage failures.

Specification (Fw 159 V2)

POWERPLANT	1 × 680hp Jumo 210Da in-line
SPAN	12.40m (40ft 7½in)
LENGTH	10.00m (32ft 9½in)
HEIGHT	3.75m (12ft 3⅜in)
WEIGHT EMPTY	1,875kg (4,134lb)
WEIGHT LOADED	2,250kg (4,960lb)
MAX SPEED	385km/h (239mph)
SERVICE CEILING	7,200m (23,622ft)
NORMAL RANGE	650km (404 miles)

Fw 187

During the late 1930s several aircraft designers turned their attentions to the production of a twin-engined single-seat fighter. Only one of these aircraft saw service in any numbers, the American-built Lockheed Lightning, although several less well known, if fascinating projects were built. It was perhaps the Dutch who produced the most radical design with the Fokker D XXIII, whilst Britain and Germany developed respectively the somewhat similar Westland Whirlwind and Focke-Wulf Fw 187.

Kurt Tank's lack of success with the Fw 159 prompted him to undertake development of a fighter which would possess a performance superior to that of any other aircraft then envisaged. To attain such a performance, he proposed the use of the still radical twin-engined single-seat layout. Although no RLM requirement existed for such a machine, Tank went ahead with detailed design work, hoping to convince the Ministry of the need for such a fighter by demonstrating its superior characteristics.

The new fighter was designed around a pair of the new 860hp Daimler Benz DB 600 in-line engines which were then under development, a maximum speed of 348mph being anticipated. After much discussion, Tank eventually succeeded in getting the RLM's Technical Department to agree to production of the aircraft, the one stipula-

Only three Fw 187A–0 pre-production aircraft were completed.

44

tion being that the less powerful Jumo 210 engines should be used in place of the DB 600s which were in very short supply.

The task of producing detailed drawings for the fighter, then designated Fw 187 and unofficially named *Falke* (Falcon) was allocated to *Ober Ing* R. Blaser. The Fw 187 was a beautifully proportioned low-wing monoplane of all-metal stressed-skin construction. A tiny fully glazed cabin was provided for the pilot in the nose of the extremely narrow section fuselage. The cabin was so tiny that some of the instruments had to be placed *outside* on the inboard sides of the engine cowlings, a similar arrangement later being adopted by the Henschel Hs 129. The two-spar wing was built in three sections and the underslung engine nacelles housed a fully retractable undercarriage.

During the late spring of 1937 the Fw 187 V1 (D–AANA) made its first flight with *Flugkapitän* Hans Sander at the controls. Sander had joined Focke-Wulf from the Rechlin experimental establishment in March 1937, taking over as chief test pilot from *Flugkapitän* Wolfgang Stein.

The Fw 187 V1 was powered by two 680hp Jumo 210Da engines driving Junkers-built Hamilton three-bladed variable pitch airscrews. Even with the reduced power provided by the Jumo engines, the aircraft attained the astonishing speed of 326mph, some 50mph faster than the Bf 109B which was just entering service. During trials, a switch was made to VDM airscrews, twin mainwheels were experimentally fitted to each undercarriage leg, and at a later stage a 7.9mm MG 17 machine-gun was mounted on either side of the cockpit.

In the summer of 1937, the Fw 187 V2

The Fw 187 A–0 shows off its ease of manoeuvrability.

joined the test programme. Essentially similar to the first aircraft, the V2 was powered by two 700hp Jumo 210G engines with fuel injection and non-retractable radiators. It also differed in having a narrower chord rudder and armament fitted as standard.

Work had just begun on the Fw 187 V3 when the decision was made to convert the aircraft into a two-seater. This was done mainly at the instigation of Ernst Udet who had just succeeded *Oberst* Wolfram von Richthofen as head of the Development Section of the RLM's Technical Department. Udet, the second highest scoring fighter ace of World War I, was firmly convinced that a twin-engined interceptor could never possess the manoeuvrability of a single-engined machine, and he therefore asked Tank to modify the Fw 187 as a two-seat destroyer or *Zerstörer*.

The second crew member, a navigator

and radio operator, was seated behind the pilot in a considerably lengthened cockpit. The provision of this second seat called for some slight modification to the fuselage, the repositioning of the fuselage fuel tank, and the lengthening of the engine bearers. The rear part of the engine nacelles was cut back and the aircraft carried an armament of two MG 17 machine-guns and two 20mm MG FF cannons.

The first two-seat version was the Fw 187 V3 (D–ORPH) which made its initial flight in the spring of 1938. It was followed by the V4 (D–OSNP) and V5 (D–OTGN) during the summer and autumn of 1938, both aircraft differing solely in having a free-blown windscreen. Previously, on May 14th, 1938, the aircraft had suffered a setback when the V1, piloted by an ex-parachute instructor named Bauer, had stalled and spun into the ground after the pilot had attempted to

All three Fw 187A–Os were painted in false operational markings in a successful attempt to deceive Allied intelligence into thinking that the machine was in Luftwaffe service.

pull the aircraft up too steeply from a high-speed run.

Despite this disaster, Tank was at last given a pair of Daimler Benz DB 600A engines which now developed 1,000hp for take-off. These were installed in the Fw 187 V6 which, although a two-seater, attained the phenomenal speed of 395mph. The aircraft was experimentally fitted with surface evaporation cooling in place of standard radiators, but although considerably reducing drag, this did cause considerable overheating problems.

A batch of three Fw 187A–0 pre-production aircraft were delivered during the summer of 1939. These were generally similar to the V4 and V5, but had an extra pair of MG 17 machine-guns and full operational equipment. Despite the excellent performance displayed by the Fw 187, the type was finally abandoned late in 1939, the RLM considering that the Bf 110

already fulfilled the rôle for which the Focke-Wulf machine was designed.

Although no production of the Fw 187 was undertaken, the three A–0s were used by an 'industrial squadron' defending the Focke-Wulf plant at Bremen in 1940, and were later transferred to Norway for use by 13.(*Zerstörer*)/JG 77. During 1942, at least one Fw 187A–0 was loaned to the *Luftschiesschule* (air gunnery school) at Vaerløse in Denmark.

Specification (Fw 187A–0)

POWERPLANTS	2 × 700hp Jumo 210G in-lines
SPAN	15.30m (50ft 2⅓in)
LENGTH	11.01m (36ft 5in)
HEIGHT	3.85m (12ft 7in)
EMPTY WEIGHT	3,600kg (8,157lb)
WEIGHT LOADED	5,000kg (11,023lb)
MAX SPEED	525km/h (326mph)
SERVICE CEILING	10,000m (32,811ft)

Fw 189 Uhu

For some reason the short-range reconnaissance machine seems one of the least interesting of all military aircraft types. It was, none the less, true that this type of aircraft was one of the most important in the Luftwaffe when one considers that the arm was basically a tactical force supporting the Wehrmacht. With that accepted, it is perhaps surprising that only two German aircraft of the type were to achieve prominence during World War II, the Hs 126 and the Fw 189 *Uhu*.

In February 1937 the RLM issued an advanced specification calling for a short-range reconnaissance aircraft to supplement and eventually replace the Hs 126 which was then undergoing trials. An important requirement of the specification was that the aircraft should possess good all-round visibility and defensive cover. Three companies were invited to submit proposals, Arado, the Hamburger Flugzeugbau and Focke-Wulf.

The Arado proposal, the Ar 198 was certainly the most conventional, being a shoulder-wing monoplane with a deep section fuselage, the underside of which was extensively glazed to provide the crew with a view of the ground. Hamburger Flugzeugbau's proposal, the Ha 141 was a most unusual design with an asymmetric layout. The crew were seated in a large extensively glazed gondola on one side of the wing centre line, a large fuselage boom incorporating the single radial engine and supporting the conventional tail surfaces, being positioned opposite. Eventually thirteen Blohm und Voss Bv 141s (as the aircraft was later redesignated) were delivered, but it proved too unconventional for the RLM.

Appearing midway between the other two proposals, the Focke-Wulf Fw 189 *Uhu* (Owl) was a low-wing monoplane with a central fuselage pod and twin booms, each supporting a 430hp Argus As 410 twelve-cylinder air-cooled engine and a large tailplane. The fuselage nacelle was extensively glazed and seated a crew of three, pilot, navigator/radio operator and flight mechanic/rear gunner. All-metal stressed skin construction was used throughout apart from the flaps and control surfaces which were fabric covered. The mainwheels retracted hydraulically into the tailbooms and a single tailwheel was provided beneath the starboard boom.

The Focke-Wulf Fw 189 was designed by *Dipl Ing* Kurt Tank, the task of producing the prototypes being placed under the control of *Dipl Ing* E. Kosel. Construction of the Fw 189 V1 (D-OPVN) began in April 1937, the prototype making its first flight in July 1938 with Kurt Tank at the controls. This aircraft and the Fw 189 V2, which flew in August, and the V3 which flew in September, proved to have excellent handling characteristics.

The second aircraft (D-OVHD) differed in carrying an armament of one flexible 7.9mm MG 15 machine-gun in the nose, dorsal and tail positions, two fixed MG 17 weapons of similar calibre being mounted in the wing roots. Four ETC 50 racks were mounted beneath the wings, each capable of carrying a 110lb bomb. The Fw 189 V3 (D-ORMH) was unarmed, but introduced the special Argus designed automatic variable-pitch airscrews which were operated by air pressure.

The twin boom layout of the Fw 189A-1 reconnaissance aircraft was chosen in order to afford the crew maximum visibility.

Following the successful testing of the three Fw 189 prototypes and because of the poor performance of the Ar 198, the RLM awarded Focke-Wulf a development contract for the *Uhu*. Late in 1938 the Fw 189 V4 (D-OCHO) production prototype made its first flight. Intended as the forerunner fo the Fw 189A series, this prototype carried full armament and was used as a test vehicle for the S 125 smoke-laying equipment and the 'Yellow Cross' group of mustard gas bombs.

Early in 1939 the Fw 189 V5 made its first flight. This featured an entirely redesigned fuselage nacelle with dual controls and was intended as the forerunner of the proposed Fw 189B trainer. The new nacelle was a smoothly streamlined structure with a stepped cockpit and a small glazed panel at the rear. Provision was made for an instructor and up to four pupils. A batch of three Fw 189B-0 pre-production and ten B-1 production aircraft were completed between late 1939 and February 1940.

Just after the last Fw 189B-1 had been delivered, Focke-Wulf received instructions to commence production of the A-series reconnaissance aircraft. During the spring of 1940 the company's Bremen assembly line completed a batch of ten Fw 189A-0 pre-production aircraft followed by 20 A-1s before the end of the year. The Fw 189A-1 was similar to the V4, carrying an armament of four 7.9mm machine-guns, four ETC 50 bomb racks and one Rb 20/30 camera. It was powered by two 465hp Argus As 410A-1 engines, introduced twin oleo legs for the mainwheels and featured a retractable tailwheel which folded into the underside of the tailplane.

Late in 1938 the Fw 189 V1 was withdrawn from the test programme and modified for use as a two-seat close support and ground attack aircraft. The fuselage nacelle was replaced by a tiny structure constructed entirely of armour plate. The pilot and gunner were seated back to back, the pilot's view being restricted to five tiny armoured glass panels. After flight trials recommenced during the spring of 1939, it was found that the tiny nacelle of the Fw 189 V1b as the aircraft was redesignated, radically altered flight characteristics, so that response to the controls became extremely sluggish.

This, coupled with the extremely poor view for both pilot and gunner, led to the Fw 189 V1b being returned to the experimental shop. Here it was again modified, the armoured glass panels being enlarged and a new gunner's position being provided. The aircraft then undertook comparative tests with the Hs 129 V2 and V3, but it was found that all three aircraft possessed extremely poor handling characteristics. Eventually the Fw 189 V1b was written-off in a crash and replaced by the Fw 189 V6, prototype for the proposed C-series. This aircraft was essentially similar to the V1b, carrying an armament of two 20mm MG FF cannon, four 7.9mm MG 17 and two 7.9mm MG 81 machine-guns. Despite possessing slightly better flight characteristics than the Hs 129, the FW 189C was abandoned in favour of its smaller and cheaper rival.

A number of additional *Uhu* prototypes were constructed, the Fw 189 V7 being the forerunner of the proposed D-series trainer floatplane. This was basically similar to the Fw 189 V5 apart from being fitted with twin floats. The Fw 189 V7 was abandoned before completion, the frame being modified to Fw 189B–0 standards.

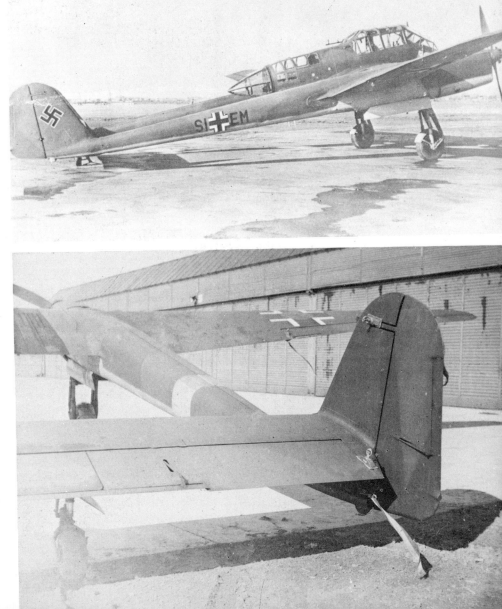

48

Below: This Fw 189A-2 carries a smoke laying canister beneath its wing on specially modified ETC 50/VIIId bomb racks.

Bottom: The Fw 189 V1b (D-OPVN) after modification as a ground attack aircraft with a heavily armoured crew nacelle.

During the spring of 1940 a number of Fw 189B–0s were delivered to the evaluation squadron 9.(H)/LG 2, followed during the autumn of the same year by a few Fw 189A–0s. However, despite the improved performance which the *Uhu* exhibited over the Hs 126, it was not until late 1941 that the aircraft began to enter service with the Luftwaffe. The first squadron to receive the machine was 2.(F)/11 based in Russia followed by *Aufklärungsgruppe* 10 *Tannenberg* and 4.(H)/31.

Two specialised transport versions of the *Uhu* were produced under the designations Fw 189A–1/U2 (w/nr 0159) and A–1/U3 (w/nr 0178), these being intended for use respectively by Generals Kesselring and Jeschonnek. The Fw 189A–2, which appeared during the summer of 1941, differed from the first production aircraft in carrying a twin 7.9mm MG 81Z gun in both the dorsal and tail positions. This installation was first tested by the Fw 189 V9 (w/nr 0030). The Fw 189A–3 was a dual-control trainer variant built in small numbers and the A–4 (introduced late in 1942) carried two 20mm MG FF cannon in place of the MG 17 machine-guns.

During 1942, production of the FW 189 switched from the Bremen complex to the Aero factory in Czechoslovakia and an assembly plant at Bordeaux-Merignac. By spring of 1943, the French plant was the sole source of supply.

Development of the basic airframe continued with the Fw 189 V10 (w/nr 0047) which was fitted with an electrically-operated undercarriage. The Fw 189 V11 (w/nr 0048) was similar but was intended as a development aircraft for the Fw

49

The Fw 189 V1b served as a prototype for the proposed Fw 189C.

The Fw 189 V1b served as a prototype for the proposed Fw 189C.

189E-0. This variant was to be powered by two 700hp Gnome-Rhone 14M fourteen-cylinder radials; a prototype, the Fw 189 V14 (w/nr 0090), being completed from drawings produced by the SNCASO company at Chatillon-sur-Seine.

The V12 and V13 (both with electrically-operated undercarriages) were respectively development aircraft for the Fw 189F-2 and F-1 production series, to be powered by two 580hp Argus As 411MA-1 engines. This engine was first tested by the Fw 189 V15, but only 17 Fw 189F-1s were completed before production of the *Uhu* came to a halt in 1944. The proposed Fw 189G powered by 950hp Argus As 402 engines was abandoned after the failure of this advanced power unit to reach production status.

By early 1943 most of the various army co-operation (H) squadrons of the Luftwaffe's reconnaissance groups had been reformed into *Nahaufklärungsgruppen* (short-range units). The majority of these units had re-equipped with the Fw 189 although a number still retained the Hs 126, or were using reconnaissance versions of the Bf 110. Apart from widespread operations in Russia, two other squadrons were equipped with the Fw 189, 1.(H)/32 in the far north and 4.(H)/12 in the western desert. Apart from use by the Luftwaffe, a number of Fw 189s were delivered to the Hungarian and Slovakian air arms.

During operations the *Uhu* was to prove an extremely tough and agile adversary, often evading attacks by considerably faster enemy fighters. Its defensive armament of six machine-guns was enough to daunt all but the most determined opponents, and its considerable structural strength enabled it to return successfully to base after being heavily damaged. The Fw 189 remained operational in small numbers until the end of the war in Europe.

Specification (Fw 189A-1)

POWERPLANTS	2 × 465hp Argus As As 410A-1 in-lines
SPAN	18.40m (60ft 4½in)
LENGTH	11.90m (39ft 5½in)
HEIGHT	3.10m (10ft 2in)
WEIGHT EMPTY	2,805kg (6,185lb)
WEIGHT LOADED	3.950kg (8,708lb)
MAX SPEED	334km/h (208mph)
SERVICE CEILING	7,000m (22,967ft)
NORMAL RANGE	670km (416 miles)

Fw 190A

During the spring of 1938, the RLM asked Focke-Wulf to undertake development of a single-engined fighter as a back-up for the Messerschmitt Bf 109. The company's chief designer, *Dipl Ing* Kurt Tank, submitted two main proposals, one powered by a liquid cooled engine and one by the new BMW 139 radial.

At first the RLM were not enthusiastic about the radial-engined machine, but Tank pointed out that the BMW unit was already offering considerably more power than the contemporary DB 601 and Jumo 211, that it was likely to be more readily available than the other two designs, and that it was much less vulnerable to battle damage.

The RLM finally chose the BMW 139 engined version of the fighter during the summer of 1938, allocating the designation Fw 190. The task of producing detailed drawings for the aircraft, unofficially dubbed *Würger* (Shrike) by Focke-Wulf, devolved upon a small team headed by *Ober Ing* R. Blaser. The team also included *Ober Ing* Mittelhuber, chief of the project office.

The prototype Fw 190 V1, D-OPZE, was rolled out in May 1939 to begin a series of taxying trials. A beautifully proportioned cantilever low-wing monoplane, the Fw 190 V1 was powered by a 1,550hp BMW 139 eighteen-cylinder two-row radial engine. This bulky power unit

Top right: *The Fw 190 V1 as originally flown in May 1939 with a ducted spinner.*

Bottom right: *In 1940 the ducted spinner of the Fw 190 V1 was removed and camouflage applied.*

was faired into the slim all-metal monocoque fuselage in what was surely a masterpiece of engineering. The VDM three-bladed airscrew was fitted with a large ducted spinner which provided a smooth unbroken line between it and the engine cowling.

All-metal stressed skin construction was used throughout, the wing being built in one piece. It was a two-spar structure, the main forward member being continuous. A fully retractable undercarriage was fitted, the mainwheel legs being hinged at almost mid-span to fold inwards. This arrangement proved a great advantage over the outwards retracting undercarriage of the Bf 109, especially under operational conditions. A neat two-piece cockpit canopy was provided, the fully glazed rear component sliding backwards for pilot entry.

On June 1st, 1939 the Fw 190 V1 made its first flight with *Flugkapitän* Hans Sander, Focke-Wulf's chief test pilot, at the controls. The engine was designed to be fitted with a ten-bladed cooling fan mounted inside the spinner, but this was not available for installation in the prototype. The fan, which was designed to rotate at three times propeller speed, was to cool the rear bank of engine cylinders. Its omission resulted in extremely high cockpit temperatures, a reading of 55° C being recorded. Sander himself claimed that it 'felt as though I had my feet in the fireplace'.

Despite the difficulties associated with the close proximity of the power plant to the cockpit and engine cooling problems, the Fw 190 proved to have an excellent performance. The prototype was flown five times by Sander before being transferred to the Rechlin experimental station for tests by Luftwaffe pilots. All agreed that the machine possessed excellent handling characteristics, a speed of 369mph being attained during trials.

On October 31st, 1939 the Fw 190 V2 (w/nr 0002) joined the test programme. Essentially similar to the first aircraft, the V2 was fitted with an engine-cooling fan, but this, perhaps surprisingly, proved to only marginally ease the overheating problems. After trials at Rechlin, the Fw 190 V1 was returned to Bremen for modification. The ducted spinner was removed and replaced by one of conventional design. The aircraft rejoined the test programme on January 25th, 1940, the removal of the ducted spinner having little effect on its performance.

Prior to the first flight of the Fw 190, BMW had contemplated the abandonment of the BMW 139 engine to concentrate on the heavier, but potentially more powerful, BMW 801. This fourteen-cylinder two-row design was of similar diameter to the BMW 139, but was considerably longer. The abandonment of the BMW 139 now presented Focke-Wulf with a considerable design problem.

Apart from introducing the larger wing, the Fw 190 V5 was the first machine to be fitted with the BMW 801 radial engine.

The Fw 190 V3 and V4, which had been designed around the BMW 139, were abandoned before completion, work being switched to a BMW 801 engined prototype, the Fw 190 V5. The installation of this engine necessitated considerable structural strengthening, the moving of the cockpit further aft, and some modification to the rudder and undercarriage. The BMW 801 produced 1,600hp for take-off, but its heavier weight, with the consequent structural strengthening of the airframe, had an obvious deleterious effect on performance, and forced Focke-Wulf to develop an entirely new wing and tailplane.

The area of the new wing was increased from 160.4 to 196.5sq ft, the surface being first fitted to the rebuilt Fw 190 V5. Now designated V5g ('g' for *grosser Flügel* or large wing), the aircraft proved only 6mph slower than its original form, but exhibited much improved climb, roll and general handling characteristics. The V6 was similar to the original Fw 190 V5 (retrospectively designated V5k—'k' for *kleiner Flügel* or small wing), but the V7 was fitted with four 7.9mm MG 17 machine-guns.

A batch of forty Fw 190A–0 pre-production aircraft was laid down at Bremen, the first machine (w/nr 0008)

leaving the assembly line in November 1940. The first seven aircraft were fitted with the small wing, but all subsequent machines, commencing with the Fw 190A–08 (w/nr 0015) had the large surface. The Fw 190 V8 (w/nr 0022) was an armament test vehicle, two MG 17 machine-guns being mounted above the engine cowling with a 20mm MG FF cannon in each wing root.

From late February 1941 six Fw 190A–0s were delivered to *Erprobungskommando* 190 under *Oblt* Otto Behrens at Rechlin for operational trials. Next month, a number of personnel from II./JG 26

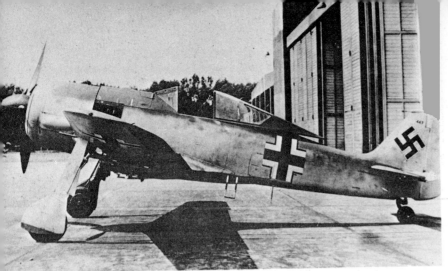

A standard production Fw 190A–3/U3 fighter-bomber (w/nr 447) during the summer of 1942.

One of the later Fw 190A–O pre-production aircraft which were tested by II./JG 26 at Maldeghem in Belgium.

arrived at Rechlin with the task of introducing the fighter into service. During the summer the programme was transferred to Le Bourget, but engine overheating problems continued to manifest themselves. It was not unusual for the engine to seize during flight, or even prior to take-off.

After much argument between Focke-Wulf and BMW, no less than fifty minor modifications were carried out on the design and eventually the special *Kommandogeräte* control gear was developed. This advanced piece of electro-hydraulically operated equipment automatically regulated airscrew pitch, fuel mixture settings, ignition and supercharger control. It eventually increased the service life of the BMW 801 from 20 to 200 hours between major overhauls.

A batch of 100 Fw 190A–1 production

aircraft ordered from the Focke-Wulf plant at Marienburg began to reach the Luftwaffe in July 1941. The Fw 190A–1 carried a similar armament to the A–0, although some aircraft were later fitted with two 20mm MG FF cannon, but the A–2 carried two MG 17 guns and two 20mm MG 151/20 cannon. Many aircraft were subsequently fitted with an additional pair of MG FF cannon in the outboard wing positions. Production of the fighter was now increasing rapidly, deliveries being received from the Ago plant at Oschersleben and the Arado factory at Warnemünde.

Early in August 1941 the first Fw 190A–1s began to replace the Bf 109E–7s in service with 6./JG 26 under *Oblt* Walter Schneider. By September the whole of II.*Gruppe* had been equipped with the aircraft, the first

clash with RAF fighters coming later in the month when three Spitfires were shot down. At first the Fw 190 was incorrectly identified as captured French Curtiss Hawk 75As, but the performance of Tank's superb fighter soon forced the RAF to think again.

The *Geschwader* staff flight of JG 26 received its first Fw 190A–1s in November 1941 and by early 1942 the whole of the wing was re-equipped with the new fighter. Early combat demonstrated that the Fw 190 was superior on almost every count to the Spitfire V and forced the hurried introduction of the Typhoon and Spitfire IX within the RAF.

During the early dogfights between RAF fighters and the Fw 190, it was not unusual for the German aircraft to flick on to its back from a very tight turn and

This Fw 190A had an ER 4 supplementary bomb rack mounted beneath the normal ETC 501 weapon carrier. This rack could carry four 110lb SC 50 bombs.

The Fw 190A–5/U3 which could carry a 2,200lb bomb and two 66 Imp gallon drop tanks on Messerschmitt designed racks.

crash at full throttle into the sea. The cause of this unpromising behaviour was the pilot making continuous use of the electrically-operated tail trimmer, an ingenious invention of Focke-Wulf, in an attempt to tighten an already high 'g' turn. The aircraft would eventually encounter a high-speed stall and flick violently, the altitude often being too low to allow the pilot to recover.

The first major action in which the Fw 190 was involved came on February 12th, 1942 when three German fighter wings provided aerial cover for the battleships *Gneisenau* and *Scharnhorst* and heavy cruiser *Prinz Eugen* attempting to break out of Brest. Apart from JG 26, equipped in the main with the Fw 190, JG 1 and 2 with the Bf 109 took part in the operation. A series of aerial battles developed over the ships, perhaps the most famous being that involving the six Swordfish torpedo bombers led by Lt Cdr Esmonde. Although the RAF suffered heavy losses, JG 26 lost only four fighters, three of these Fw 190A–2s from 8. and 9.*Staffeln*.

About 400 Fw 190A–2s were completed before production switched to the more powerful A–3. This variant was powered by the 1,700hp BMW 801D–2 radial, several early Fw 190s, including the V6 and V8, having been fitted with this unit in the spring of 1942. Apart from the engine, the Fw 190A–3 also introduced a standard armament of two MG 17 machine-guns in the upper fuselage decking, two MG 151/20 cannon in the wing roots and two MG FF weapons in the wings outboard of the undercarriage.

A number of conversions of the basic model were produced including the Fw 190A–3/U1 and U3 fighter-bombers, the A–3/U4 fighter reconnaissance aircraft, and the A–3/U7 ground-attack project. Most of these conversions involved the removal of the outboard MG FF cannon and replacement by ETC 500 bomb racks or Rb 12 5/7 × 9 cameras.

Delivery of the Fw 190A–4 began in the summer of 1942, this variant having provision for MW–50 water-methanol injection and FuG 16Z radio equipment. The only external difference between the A–3 and A–4 was the small aerial pylon on top of the fin necessitated by the new radio type. Variations on the basic theme included the A–4/U1, U3 and U8 fighter-bombers and the A–4/R6 bomber destroyer with two 210mm rocket tubes underwing.

By the middle of 1942, the three main

55

fighter units in the west, JG 1, 2 and 26 were almost completely re-equipped with the Fw 190A-2 and A-3. The recently established fighter-bomber squadrons, 10.(Jabo)/JG 2 and JG 26 also began to receive the Fw 190A-3/U1. These units operated low-level sneak raids over the south coast of the British Isles, and were eventually expanded to form the Fw 190 equipped fast bomber wing, SKG 10. III./SKG 10 was formed from III./ZG 2 in the middle east in December 1942 and was joined by two other *Gruppen* in February 1943 and by IV./SKG 10 in April.

An attempt had been made to equip II./JG 54 with the Fw 190 on the eastern front in November 1941, but failed owing to the engine overheating problems that were being experienced at that time. The first machines to operate successfully on the eastern front were delivered to I./JG 51 under *Hptm* Heinrich Krafft in August 1942. By February 1943 both III. and

IV./JG 51, under the overall command of *Maj* Friedrich Beckh, had received the type together with I./JG 54 in northern Russia.

Apart from conventional fighter units, the Fw 190 was also being delivered to the ground-attack groups I. and II./Sch.G 1 in the Crimea and I./Sch.G 2 in North Africa, and the reconnaissance squadrons NAGr 13 and 4. and 5.(F)/123, all operating on the western front for short-range observation of the British Isles.

In April 1943, the Fw 190A-5 began to replace the A-4 on the production line. The new variant differed in having a longer engine cowling, this feature increasing overall length by almost 6 inches. A large number of sub-variants were completed, the modifications mainly concerning armament. The A-5/U2, U8 and U13 were long-range fighter-bombers, the A-5/U3 could carry a 2,200lb bomb load and the A-5/U4 was a reconnaissance machine with provision for two Rb 12 cameras. The

Fw 190A-5/U9 and U12 were destroyers with provision for two MG 131 machine-guns and four MG 151/20 cannon in various arrangements. The A-5/U11 and U17 were ground-attack types, the former carrying two 30mm MK 103 cannon, and the U14 and U15 were torpedo-bombers. Three torpedo-carrying Fw 190s were delivered to III./KG 200 under *Maj* Helmut Viedebantt early in 1945.

The Fw 190A-5/U10 tested a modified wing which had been developed for the Fw 190A-6. The latter variant was delivered from June 1943, having provision for a number of *Rüstsätze* conversion packs. Eventually no less than 31 of these packs were developed for the Fw 190 and Ta 152, most of them being in the form of additional armament, radio or power-boosting equipment. Aircraft fitted with tropical filters were identified by the suffix 'trop'.

On January 27th, 1943, the USAAF mounted its first big daylight raid on

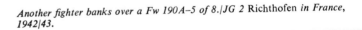

A Fw 190A-4 fighter possibly of the staff flight of JG 2 on the Channel Coast, summer 1942.

Another fighter banks over a Fw 190A-5 of 8./JG 2 Richthofen *in France, 1942/43.*

Germany, the only Luftwaffe fighters to intercept being a few Fw 190s from JG 1. Reaction to these raids was swift, the Luftwaffe establishing a new wing, JG 11, by the splitting of JG 1; and the transferring of JG 3, II./JG 27 and III./JG 54 to Germany. Towards the middle of 1943, a gradual switch was made to the improved versions of the Bf 109G which were beginning to enter service. By August only six day fighter groups were equipped with the Fw 190 on the western front. These were I. and II./JG 1, I. and III./JG 2, I./JG 11 and I./JG 26.

The USAAF made the first of their shuttle bombing attacks on August 17th, 1943, taking off from Britain, attacking the Messerschmitt factory at Regensburg, and landing in North Africa. Soon after crossing the Dutch coast they were shadowed by Fw 190s from II./JG 1 and attacked along about 150 miles of their route. Virtually every Luftwaffe fighter unit in the west took part in the operation, using machine-guns, cannon and 210mm rockets to combat the American bombers. The fighters of JG 1 and JG 11 moved almost 250 miles to join the fight.

Earlier, in July 1943, *Maj* Hajo Herrmann proposed the establishment of a number of single-engined fighter units to supplement the operations of the conventional night interceptors. An experimental unit was established under the designation *Kommando Herrmann*, and its success led to the formation of a complete wing known as JG 300. The *Stab* and II.*Gruppe* were equipped with the Fw 190, and were later joined by two other wings designated JG 301 and 302.

Initial operations were quite successful, but with the onset of winter losses rose alarmingly. By December 1943, nine FW 190 equipped fighter units were operating in the defence of Germany. These were I. and II./JG 1, III. and 10./JG 11, III./JG 54, II./JG 300, II./JG 302 and *Sturmstaffel 1*. In the west I. and III./JG 2 and I. and II./JG 26 were operational, whilst I., II. and IV./JG 54 were using the machine on the eastern front.

Development of the basic airframe continued, although only about 80 of the Fw 190A–7 variant were built, the type having two 13mm MG 131 machine-guns mounted above the engine cowling, FuG 16ZE and FuG 25 radio equipment and Revi 16ʰ gunsight. The majority of A–7s were completed by the Fieseler company at Kassel, deliveries beginning in December 1943.

The next variant, the Fw 190A–8, was built in larger numbers than any other. The type was similar to the A–7, but had provision for MW–50 water-methanol injection, FuG 16ZY radio equipment and the repositioning of the ETC 501 bomb rack. The Fw 190A–8 was built by Focke-Wulf at Marienburg, Posen, Cottbus and

A Fw 190A Jabo (fighter-bomber) carrying an unusually marked 1,100lb SC 500 bomb.

The Fw 190A–8 was experimentally fitted with eight 110lb SC 50 bombs, four beneath the wings and four below the fuselage.

Sorau, Ago at Oschersleben, Arado at Warnemünde, Fieseler at Kassel-Waldau, Dornier at Wismar and the Weserflugzeugbau. A large series of *Rüstsätze* conversion packs were produced for the variant including the A-8/R7 heavily armoured fighter intended for use by the *Sturmstaffeln*.

A two-seat training version of the Fw 190A-8 was completed under the designation A-8/U1, but no large-scale production of the Fw 190S-5 and S-8, respectively two-seat versions of the A-5 and A-8, was undertaken. One of the A-8/U1s was delivered to a ground-attack training unit, possibly SG 151, whilst another was captured by Allied forces in France.

The final production version of the A-series was the Fw 190A-9 to be powered by the 2,000hp BMW 801F engine. The A-9 was intended for use by the *Sturmstaffeln*, having considerable armour protection for the pilot. Production of the type was scheduled to begin in September 1944, but in the event only a prototype, the Fw 190 V34, was completed. The existence of the Fw 190A-10 project powered by the BMW 801F engine has yet to be confirmed.

On February 20th, 1944, the USAAF launched the first of its 'Big Week' attacks designed to wreck the German aircraft industry. On the first day of the assault, almost 1,000 American bombers were directed against Bf 109 assembly plants near Leipzig. For the loss of 21 bombers, the USAAF destroyed 23 Luftwaffe fighters and 15 destroyers. Little damage was caused to German assembly plants on February 21st, although the Luftwaffe lost a total of 23 aircraft.

The Junkers factories in and around Bernburg provided the targets for the attacks of February 22nd, the USAAF bombers being attacked continuously throughout the operation. Eventually 41 aircraft were destroyed for the loss of 35 German fighters. Bad weather prevented extensive operations on 23rd, but on February 24th, the day when JG 26 claimed its 2,000th victory, a heavy force attacked the Bf 110 factories at Gotha. The bombers were intercepted some 80 minutes from the target and the loss of 49 aircraft was eventually reported. A total of 36 Luftwaffe were destroyed in the air, 34 of them single-engine fighters. The final mission took place on February 25th when over 800 bombers attacked Messerschmitt factories near Augsburg. The Luftwaffe lost a total of 22 fighters for the destruction of 31 bombers.

Despite the heavy blow against the

This photo of the Fw 190A-8 (w/nr 0022) shows the aircraft fitted with a single 550lb SC 250 bomb.

German aircraft industry, production of the Bf 109 and Fw 190 continued to increase. This was mainly due to the efforts of *Reichsminister* Albert Speer and the *Jägerstab*. Monthly production figures for the Fw 190 were 209 in February 1944, 373 in March, 461 in April, 482 in May and 689 in June.

When the Allies invaded Normandy on June 6th, 1944, the only German fighters to appear over the beach-head were the Fw 190s of *Oberstlt* Josef Priller, commander of JG 26, and his wingman. The front was rapidly reinforced, and by June 10th, nine Fw 190 equipped groups were moved to France. These were I./JG 1 at Le Mans, II./JG 1 at Flers, I. and III./JG 2 at Cormeilles, IV.(*Sturm*)/JG 3 at St Andre, I./JG 11 at Rennes, I./JG 26 around Lille, II./JG 26 at Cambrai and III./JG 54 at Chartres.

During late April 1944, *Sturmstaffel 1* was incorporated into IV./JG 3 and the complete *Gruppe* re-equipped with the Fw 190. The pilots of the newly created *Sturmgruppe* of JG 3 were pledged to destroy an enemy bomber during every mission, either by conventional means, or failing that, by ramming. After a short period at the invasion front, IV.(*Sturm*)/JG 3 under *Hptm* Wilhelm Moritz was transferred back to Germany, where it operated with an escort provided by I. and II./JG 300. The unit's most successful operation was on July 7th, 1944 when it claimed the destruction of 30 bombers.

Later in July, II./JG 300 under *Maj* Kurd Peters re-equipped with the Fw 190 as a *Sturmgruppe*, the Bf 109Gs of I. and III./JG 300 providing fighter escort. A third unit was established in August 1944 from a combination of the *Rammstaffel*

and I./ZG 1. Designated II.(*Sturm*)/JG 4 the *Gruppe* was commanded by *Maj* Hans-Günther von Kornatzki. On October 6th, IV./(*Sturm*)/JG 3 returned to its parent *Geschwader* and nine days later IV.(*Sturm*)/JG 300 was established from part of ZG 76. With the increase in American fighter escort, the *Sturm* units suffered heavily, IV./JG 3 losing 15 pilots in August 1944, and by November *Maj* Moritz was forced to give up his command owing to complete exhaustion.

A large variety of armaments were tested by the Fw 190A including the SG series of special weapons and the X–4 missile. The SG 116 *Zellendusche* comprised three, four or six 30mm MK 103 gun barrels arranged to fire upwards at an angle of approximately 73°. The device was triggered via a photo-electric cell by the shadow of the bomber passing over-

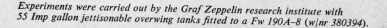

Experiments were carried out by the Graf Zeppelin research institute with 55 Imp gallon jettisonable overwing tanks fitted to a Fw 190A-8 (w/nr 380394).

head. Tests with this installation were carried out by the experimental fighter unit, JGr 10 under *Maj* Georg Cristl using a Fw 58 and He 177 as target aircraft.

The Fw 190 V74 was used to test the SG 117 *Röhrblock* weapon which comprised seven 30mm MK 108 barrels clustered together to fire upwards at a bomber. Beside the 210mm WGr 21 rockets mentioned earlier, the Fw 190 also tested the 280mm WGr 28 missile and 55mm R4M projectiles. Perhaps the most interesting air-to-air weapon tested by the Fw 190 was the X–4 *Ruhrstahl* wire-guided missile with a BMW 109–548 rocket engine. Two of these weapons were mounted beneath the wing of a Fw 190A–8.

Towards the end of 1944, the Fw 190A was beginning to be replaced by the long-nosed Fw 190D. The supply of aviation fuel to the Luftwaffe was rapidly becoming exhausted and with the approach of Allied ground forces, Germany was nearing collapse. After the mass attack on Allied airfields on January 1st, 1945, very few German piston-engined fighters were encountered by the Allied air forces, and most Fw 190s ended their days in neat impotent rows on Luftwaffe airfields.

Specification (Fw 190A–8)

POWERPLANT	1 × 1,700hp BMW 801D–2 radial
SPAN	10.50m (34ft 5½in)
LENGTH	8.84m (29ft 0in)
HEIGHT	3.96m (12ft 11¾in)
WEIGHT EMPTY	3,175kg (7,011lb)
WEIGHT LOADED	4,900kg (10,805lb)
MAX SPEED	654km/h (408mph)
SERVICE CEILING	11,400m (37,403ft)
NORMAL RANGE	800km (497 miles)

Above left: *Tests were carried out with a special flame damping exhaust system for night flying Fw 190As.*

Above right: *Another view of the Fw 190A–8 (w/nr 380394) which was operationally tested by VJGr 10.*

Fw 190B and C

Although a very effective fighter at altitudes below 20,000ft, the performance of the Fw 190A tended to fall off rapidly above that height. Therefore, during 1942, consideration was given to improving the performance of the fighter, particularly at altitude. Three proposals were made; the Fw 190B powered by the BMW 801 engine, the Fw 190C with the DB 603 unit and the Fw 190D with the Jumo 213.

The first prototype of the B-series was the Fw 190 V13 (w/nr 0036) which was powered by a BMW 801C-1 radial with the GM-1 power boosting system. The system involved the injection of nitrous oxide into the engine where it provided additional oxygen for combustion. Despite the increase in performance which the GM-1 system conferred, it was very heavy, and its pressurised tanks were extremely vulnerable to battle damage.

Four additional B-series aircraft were completed, the V24 and w/nrs 0047, 0048 and 0049, all being fitted with pressurised cabins, BMW 801D engines with GM-1 and broader fin and rudder assemblies. The Fw 190 V24 also introduced a larger wing with a span of 35ft 7in. Trials indicated that the overall increase in performance offered by the Fw 190B-0 was not sufficient to warrant production. Therefore it, and the proposed Fw 190B-1, B-1/R1 and B-2 were abandoned in favour of the Fw 190C.

The Fw 190 V13's BMW 801C engine was removed and replaced by a 1,750hp Daimler Benz DB 603A-0 twelve-cylinder unit. The Fw 190 V16 and V18 (the latter being the first true C-series machine) were

The Fw 190 V13 (w/nr 0036), first prototype for the B-series after the installation of the DB 603A engine.

also powered by DB 603 engines, the former aircraft attaining a speed of 450mph with the aid of MW-50 water-methanol injection during trials.

Late in 1942 the TK 11 turbo-supercharger developed by the DVL became available to Focke-Wulf engineers. The TK 11 was mounted below the fuselage of the Fw 190 V18 and enclosed by a large ventral fairing which resulted in the nickname of *Kanguruh* (Kangaroo). Apart from the supercharger, the modified prototype, now known as the V18/U1, also differed in having a DB 603G engine driving a four-bladed wooden airscrew and the broader fin and rudder first tested by the four B-series prototypes.

The V25 to V28, which were B- and C-series development aircraft, were followed by five true Fw 190C-0s. Generally

similar to the V18/U1, these were the V29 and V30 fitted with Hirth 2281 turbo-superchargers and the V31 to V33 fitted with the TK 11 installation. Protracted development work was carried out with these aircraft, but the superchargers suffered constant failures, the V31 eventually crashing on April 29th, 1943.

At one stage in their careers, all six Fw 190Cs were fitted with a pressurised cabin. The canopy was of the same outline as the normal structure apart from two bracing ribs, but was double glazed. The side windows had warm air circulated through them to assist in heating the pilot's enclosure. Despite intensive work carried out with the pressurised cabin, this too proved extremely vulnerable to failure. The sharp edges of the cockpit frame cut into the sealing compounds, the valves failed to seat properly, and in several cases the glass itself shattered under pressure.

By the beginning of 1944, it was becoming obvious that the Fw 190C would still have to undergo intensive development before it could be used operationally. This, combined with the fact that the Jumo 213 powered Fw 190D–9 was nearing the mass production stage, forced Focke-Wulf to adandon further work on the sub-type.

Specification (Fw 190C–0)

POWERPLANT	1 × 1,900hp DB 603G in-line
SPAN	10.50m (34ft 5½in)
LENGTH	9.75m (32ft 0in)
HEIGHT	3.96m (12ft 11¾in)
MAX SPEED	668km/h (415mph)
SERVICE CEILING	12,000m (39,372ft)

The first genuine C-series aircraft was the Fw 190 V18 (w/nr 0040), seen here in its V18/U1 form with a TK 11 turbo-supercharger.

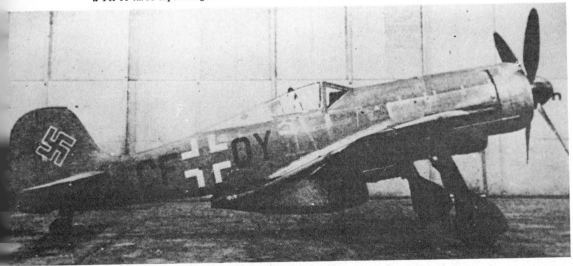

Fw 190D

Despite the intensive development work carried out on the Fw 190B and C series, it was not until the appearance of the Fw 190D that an overall improvement in the performance of Tank's superb fighter was attained. The Fw 190D was basically the airframe of the Fw 190A married to a 1,750hp Junkers Jumo 213 twelve-cylinder in-line engine. Although very successful, the fighter was regarded by Tank as a stop gap pending the arrival of the Ta 152.

In March 1942 a Fw 190A–0 (w/nr 0039) was fitted with a Jumo 213A engine as the Fw 190 V17, and during the mid-summer a further five prototypes, the V20, V21, V22, V23 and V25 were similarly modified. The installation of the Jumo engine necessitated a 2ft increase in the length of the nose, with a compensating parallel section added immediately forward of the tail fin.

During the autumn of 1943 a Fw 190A–7 was taken from the production line and fitted with a Jumo 213A engine as the Fw 190 V53, first of a small series of D–0 pre-production aircraft. In May 1944 the Fw 190 V17 was modified as the forerunner of the proposed Fw 190D–9 production series under the designation V17/U1.

The production prototype for the D–9 was the Fw 190 V54 (w/nr 170024) which featured an increase in tail fin area to compensate for some longitudinal instability. The V54 carried an armament of two 20mm MG 151/20 cannon in the wing roots and two 13mm MG 131 mounted above the engine cowling. An ETC 504 bomb rack was positioned below the fuselage with two ETC 71 or ETC 503 racks beneath the wings. The V53 and V54 were successfully tested during the summer of 1944, but production was delayed after both prototypes were damaged in an Allied bombing attack on Langenhagen.

Deliveries of the Fw 190D–9 began in August 1944, the first production aircraft from the Cottbus assembly line receiving constructor's numbers in the 210000 series. A second production line was established at the Fieseler plant at Kassel-Waldau. Early versions of the Fw 190D–9 featured the original type cockpit hood, but this was soon changed to the bubble canopy first introduced by the Fw 190F series.

The first Luftwaffe unit to receive the 'Dora 9' as the aircraft was quickly nicknamed was III./JG 54 under *Maj* Robert 'Bazi' Weiss. After re-equipment was completed, the unit moved to its operational bases at Hesepe and Achmer to protect the operations of the first jet fighter squadron, *Kommando Nowotny* equipped with the Me 262A–1a. The Messerschmitt fighter was at its most vulnerable when taking off and landing, and it was for this reason that III./JG 54 was brought in to protect its bases.

At first the pilots of III./JG 54 were not too enthusiastic about their new mount, and their scepticism was not helped when Tank himself pronounced that 'the Fw 190D–9 is only an interim solution until the Ta 152 comes into series production'. However during operations the 'Dora 9' proved to have much improved climb and dive characteristics, was faster than the Fw 190A–8, and could out-turn both this aircraft and the Bf 109G.

The next Luftwaffe unit to receive the Fw 190D–9 was I./JG 26 under *Maj* Karl Borris followed, early in 1945, by the remainder of the *Geschwader*. On Christmas Day 1944, III./JG 54 was placed under the control of JG 26 but four days later *Maj* Weiss and five other pilots were killed when the *Gruppe* clashed with a formation of Spitfires. *Oblt* Hans Dortenmann temporarily took over leadership of the unit, but on February 25th, 1945 it was redesignated IV./JG 26, with *Maj* Rudolf Klemm as commander.

The first two Fw 190D–9s to be com-

Top right: *A converted A–7 airframe, the Fw 190 V53 (w/nr 170003) was the first D–O series prototype. It was later modified as the V68 and served as prototype for the Ta 152B–5.*

Bottom right: *A Russian soldier stands before a Fw 190F–8 with a D–9 in the background.*

pleted (w/nrs 210001 and 210002) were converted as the sole examples of the Fw 190D–10. This differed in being powered by a Jumo 213C engine which had provision for a 30mm MK 108 cannon to be mounted between the cylinder banks, firing through the spinner. The starboard MG 151/20 gun was deleted and provision was made for MW–50 injection.

During the autumn of 1944, seven Fw 190A–8 airframes were modified as prototypes for the Fw 190D–11 under the designations V55 to V61. The Fw 190D–11 was powered by a Jumo 213F engine and carried an armament of two MG 151/20 cannon in the wing roots, and two MK 108 guns in the outboard wing positions. A number of minor modifications were produced in connection with the D-series including the R11 bad weather fighter with PKS 12 autopilot and FuG 125 blind landing radio equipment, the R20 with MW–50 injection and the PKS 12 autopilot and the R21 with FuG 125 equipment.

In February 1945 the first Fw 190D–12s appeared, this version being intended for the dual rôles of interceptor and ground attack aircraft. An armament of one engine-mounted MK 108 cannon and two wing-mounted MG 151/20 guns was carried, and increased armour protection was provided around the engine. The Fw 190D–12/R5 was powered by the Jumo 213EB engine with increased compression ratio, and the R11 and R21 conversion packs could also be fitted to the variant. The D–12/R25 also carried MW–50 injection, but differed from the R21 in having the Jumo 213EB engine. The Fw 190D–13 was merely a D–12 with the engine-mounted MK 108 cannon replaced by a MG 151/20 gun.

Two early production Fw 190D–9s (w/nrs 210040 and 210043) were taken from the production line in October 1944 and fitted with the 1,800hp DB 603E engine at the Daimler Benz test establishment at Stuttgart-Echterdingen. Trials with these prototypes, redesignated V76 and V77 respectively, indicated that a maximum speed of 435mph was attainable at altitude. The RLM immediately instructed that two DB 603 powered variants be produced under the designations Fw 190D–14 and D–15. The D–14 was to be powered by the 1,800hp DB 603E or 2,100hp DB 603LA engine and the D–15 by the 1,900hp DB 603G.

During the middle of March 1945 a batch of 15 Fw 190D–9s were delivered to Echterdingen for conversion to D–15 standard (this variant designed to precede the D–14 on the production line) but only one aircraft was completed before the arrival of American troops. About 700 Fw 190Ds had been built by this time, the Focke-Wulf plants at Marienburg and Sorau/Silesia also undertaking production of the variant.

Apart from JG 26 and III./JG 54, several other units were partially equipped with the Fw 190D–9 including JG 1, JG 2, JG 4 and JG 301. In March 1945 the whole of JG 6 *Horst Wessel* under *Maj* Gerhard Barkhorn was equipped with no less than 150 brand new Fw 190D–9s from the nearby factory at Sorau/Silesia. However, such was the shortage of fuel that the *Geschwader* was only able to mount standing patrols of four aircraft.

One of a small batch of Fw 190S–8 two-seat conversion trainers to be completed.

Specification (Fw 190D–9)

POWERPLANT	1 × 1,776hp Jumo 213A–1 in-line
SPAN	10.50m (34ft 5½in)
LENGTH	10.24m (33ft 5¼in)
HEIGHT	3.35m (11ft 0¼in)
WEIGHT EMPTY	3,590kg (7,694lb)
WEIGHT LOADED	4,300kg (9,480lb)
MAX SPEED	685km/h (426mph)
SERVICE CEILING	12,000m (39,372ft)
NORMAL RANGE	837km (520 miles)

Fw 190F and G

Towards the end of 1941, the Luftwaffe's only ground attack group was expanded to form the basis of a new wing designated Sch.G 1, a second wing being created during the late summer of 1942. Both units were equipped initially with a mixture of Bf 109s, Hs 123s, Hs 129s and Ju 87s, but towards the end of 1942, two specialised variants of the Fw 190 were developed. These two variants, the Fw 190F ground attack aircraft and the Fw 190G long-range fighter-bomber were produced in parallel; the proposed Fw 190E reconnaissance fighter having been abandoned at an early stage.

The Fw 190F-1 was a development of the A-4 with the outboard 20mm cannon deleted, an ETC 501 bomb rack under the fuselage and increased armour protection for the pilot and engine. The Fw 190F-2 was similar, based on the Fw 190A-5 airframe, but with a new blown cockpit canopy to improve the pilot's view. The Fw 190F-3 was a development of the A-6 airframe with an ETC 250 fuselage rack capable of carrying a 550lb bomb or a 66 Imp gallon drop tank. The Fw 190F-3/R1 carried four ETC 50 bomb racks beneath the wings, and the F-3/R3 two 30mm MK 103 cannon in a similar position.

The Fw 190F-4 to F-7 were abandoned in favour of the F-8 based on the Fw 190A-8 airframe. This variant carried a pair of 13mm MG 131 machine-guns above the engine cowling in place of the

Right: An operational Fw 190F-3/R1 fighter-bomber which carried an ETC 501 bomb rack beneath the fuselage and four ETC 50 weapons below the wings.

earlier 7.9mm weapons and four ETC 50 wing racks as standard. The F-8/U1 was a proposed tandem two-seat trainer and the F-8/U2 and U3 were equipped with a TSA bombsight to enable the respective launching of a 1,540lb BT 700 or 3,090lb BT 1400 anti-shipping weapon.

A large number of *Rüstsätze* conversion packs were produced for the Fw 190F-8. These included the F-8/R2 which mounted two 30mm MK 108 cannon underwing and the R3 which carried two 30mm MK 103 weapons in a similar position. The R5 featured an additional 115ltr (25 gallon) fuel tank in the rear fuselage, the R11 had all-weather capabilities and the R13 carried flame dampers, an ETC 503 bomb rack and improved radio equipment for the night ground-attack rôle. The F-8/R14, produced in prototype form as the F-8/U14, carried a LTF 5b torpedo on an ETC 502 rack and the R15 and R16 were respectively production versions of the F-8/U2 and U3 to be built by Blohm und Voss.

During the middle of 1944, the Fw 190F-8 was supplemented by the F-9 on

the production lines. The F-9 was similar to its predecessor, but was powered by a 2,000hp BMW 801TS radial. The Fw 190F-10, production of which was scheduled to commence in March 1945, introduced the 2,000hp BMW 801F engine and carried an armament of two MG 131 machine-guns, two MG 151/20 and two MK 103 cannon. Only prototypes of the Fw 190F-15 and F-16 were produced before the end of the war, these featuring modified undercarriages with large wheels, improved radio equipment, the BMW 801TS/TH engine and ETC 504 bomb racks.

The Fw 190G-1 of which 50 aircraft were completed during the winter of 1942/43, was developed from the Fw 190A-5. It could carry a 1,100kg SC 500 bomb beneath the fuselage plus two 300ltr (66 Imp gallon) drop tanks under the wings. The G-2 was similar but introduced Messerschmitt instead of Junkers designed racks for the drop tanks. The Fw 190G-3, first built in the late summer of 1943, was equipped with the

PKS 11 auto pilot, several modifications being introduced at a later stage including petrol injection, a variometer and tropical filters.

The last important version of the G-series was the Fw 190G-8, production of which was undertaken between September 1943 and February 1944. The G-8 was based on the Fw 190A-8 airframe, featuring FuG 16ZY radio equipment and the repositioning of the ETC 501 bomb rack eight inches further forward. The ETC 501 fuselage rack could accommodate a 1,100lb SC 500 bomb, and two ETC 250 wing racks mounted either a 550lb bomb or a 66 gallon drop tank. The Fw 190G-8/R1 featured MW-50 water-methanol injection and the G-8/R4 introduced the GM-1 nitrous-oxide power boosting system. The Fw 190G-8/R5 had each ETC 250 rack replaced by two ETC 50 racks, and provision for a 25 gallon auxiliary tank in each wing. The proposed Fw 190G-9, based on the A-9 airframe, was abandoned.

Apart from the armament combinations mentioned previously, the Fw 190F was used to test several radical weapons. These included the SG 113A *Försteronde* anti-tank rocket tube which fired a 77mm shell vertically downwards. Two of these weapons were mounted in each wing of three Fw 190F-8s, and during trials at the

Top right: *Czech civilians examine a damaged Fw 190G-1 fighter-bomber (w/nr 588717) of an unidentified Luftwaffe unit in May 1945.*

Bottom right: *A Fw 190F-3/R1 of the Luftwaffe. The aircraft bears the markings of III.Gruppe, but the* Geschwader *remains unidentifiable.*

Volkenrode test centre, one of these aircraft succeeded in penetrating the armour of a captured Russian T–34 tank.

Other weapons tested by the Fw 190F–8 included the X–4 and X–7 guided missiles, the *Panzerschreck* 1 and 2 anti-tank rockets and the WGr 28/32 weapon, a development of the WGr 21 air-to-air missile. Either one or two of these 280mm anti-tank rockets were mounted beneath the wing of the Fw 190F–8, but proved unsuccessful. Perhaps the most interesting weapon tested by the Fw 190F–8 however was the Blohm und Voss Bv 246 *Hagelkorn* guided glider bomb. Tests of this weapon, which was designed to be launched against enemy strongpoints and naval targets, began at Karlshagen during early July 1944, using a Fw 190F–8 (w/nr 130795). But, although

over 1,000 Bv 246s were built, the missile failed to see operational service.

In December 1942, both *Schlachtgeschwader* 1 and 2 began their re-equipment with the Fw 190. Sch.G 1 and II./Sch.G 2 were based in Russia, I./Sch.G 2 operating under *Fliegerführer Afrika* in the western desert. In October 1943, the whole of the Luftwaffe's dive bomber and ground-attack arm was reorganised, a gradual switch to the Fw 190F being made from that date. The new wings, SG 4 and SG 10, were equipped with the Fw 190 from their formation, and shortly afterwards II./SG 2 (which flew as escort for Rudel's famous III.*Gruppe*) received the machine. It was planned to re-equip one ground-attack group with the Fw 190 every six weeks, but it was not until late 1944 that production

was sufficient to make this plan practical.

After tests at Hexengrund, a number of BT 400 and BT 700 equipped Fw 190F–8s were delivered to I./SG 5 late in 1944. In November the *Gruppe*, under *Maj* Helmut Viedenbantt, was redesignated III./KG 200, moving from Norway to Berlin-Staaken for night flying training. In February 1945 the *Gruppe* became operational at Twente in Holland. Apart from the BT torpedo bombs, III./KG 200's aircraft carried a mixture of AB 250 or AB 500 weapon containers (enclosing small bombs or flares) or 2,200lb SC 1,000 bombs.

Another important ground attack unit equipped with the Fw 190 was III./KG 51 which had been formed from I./SKG 10 in August 1944. This unit, operating five Fw 190G–1s with 3,790lb SC 1,800 bombs provided by *Sonderverbänd Einhorn* (later 13./KG 200) made an attack on the Nijmegan bridge in September. Shortly afterwards the *Gruppe* was redesignated NSGr 20 under *Maj* Kurt Dahlmann, operating several further strikes against Allied held bridges during the spring of 1945. With the SC 1,800 bomb, the Fw 190G required a take-off run of at least 1,300 yards.

Specification (Fw 190F–3)

POWERPLANT	1 × 1,700hp BMW 801D–2 radial
SPAN	10.50m (34ft 5½in)
LENGTH	8.96m (29ft 4⅔in)
HEIGHT	3.96m (12ft 11¾in)
WEIGHT EMPTY	3,320kg (7,320lb)
WEIGHT LOADED	4,400kg (9,702lb)
MAX SPEED	635km/h (394mph)
MAXIMUM RANGE	750km (466 miles)

FW 190 Prototypes

The table that follows lists each known Fw 190 prototype together with its *Werke-Nummer* and brief details. Nothing is known of the Fw 190 V10, V11, V37 to V41, V43, V44, V46 and V48 to V50.

V1 0001 D–OPZE, BMW 139 engine, ducted spinner.

V2 0002 FO+LY, later RM+CA, similar to V1, 2 × MG 17 guns.

V3 0003 Not built.

V4 0004 Not built.

V5 0005 BMW 801C–0, originally V5k with small wing, later V5g with larger wing. V5g projected with skis.

V6 0006 BMW 801C–0, similar to V5k, later BMW 801D–2.

V7 0007 BMW 801C–0, similar to V5k, 4 × MG 17 guns.

V8 0022 BMW 801C–1, tested 2 × MG FF cannon, ETC 250 and ETC 500 bomb racks, later BMW 801D–2.

V9 0023 BMW 801C–1, Fw 190A–1 production prototype.

V12 0035 BMW 801C–1, fitted with pressurised cabin and special cockpit jettisoning device.

V13 0036 SK+JS, BMW 801C–1, Fw 190B series prototype, later with DB 603 engine.

V14 BMW 801C–2, Fw 190A–2 production prototype.

V15 0037 BMW 801C–2, larger wing with a span of 35ft 7in, CF+OV, later with DB 603.

V16 0038 CF+OW, second Fw 190B, DB 603A, later DB 603E V83.

V17 0039 CF+OX, first Fw 190D prototype, Jumo 213A engine, modified as V17/U1 as forerunner of the Fw 190D–9.

V18 0040 CF+OY, DB 603A engine,

A Focke-Wulf Fw 190G–1 carrying a 1,100lb SC 500 bomb prepares for take-off from a snow-covered Luftwaffe airfield.

A wide variety of experiments were carried out using Fw 190 airframes. This machine had a special oblique camera pod attached to the fuselage.

modified as V18/U1 with TK 11 super-charger, forerunner of Fw 190C, pressure cabin, modified as V18/U2, GH + KO, Jumo 213A engine, forerunner of Ta 152H–0.

V19 0041 GH + KP, Jumo 213A engine, new wing, crashed on February 16th, 1944.

V20 0042 GH + KQ, Jumo 213A, Fw 190D series prototype, modified as V20/U1, prototype for Ta 152H–0, later proposed with DB 603L engine.

V21 0043 GH + KR, Jumo 213A, larger wing, modified as V21/U1 with DB 603B, prototype for Ta 152C–0, modified again as V21/U2 with DB 603LA and engine-mounted MK 108 cannon.

V22 0044 Jumo 213A, Fw 190D series prototype.

V23 0045 Jumo 213A, Fw 190D series prototype.

V24 0046 BMW 801C, Fw 190B series prototype, larger wing, pressure cabin.

V25 0050 DB 603A engine, B/C-series aircraft, later re-engined with Jumo 213A as D-series machine.

V26 0051 DB 603A engine, B/C-series development aircraft.

V27 0052 DB 603A engine, B/C-series development aircraft.

V28 0053 DB 603A engine, B/C-series development aircraft.

V29 0054 GH + KS, DB 603G, Fw 190C series prototype, later with Hirth 2281 supercharger, modified as V29/U1 with Jumo 213A, Ta 152H–0 prototype.

V30 0055 GH + KT, DB 603G, similar to V29, later modified as V30/U1 with Jumo 213A, Ta 152H–0 prototype, crashed on August 13th, 1944.

V31 0056 GH + KU, DB 603G, Fw 190C prototype, TK 11 supercharger, crashed April 28th, 1943.

V32 0057 GH + KV, DB 603G, similar to V31, modified as V32/U1 with Jumo 213F, Ta 153 prototype, again modified as V32/U2 with Jumo 213E, Ta 152H–0 prototype.

V33 0058 GH + KW, DB 603G, similar to V31, modified as V33/U1, Ta 152H–1 prototype, crashed July 13th, 1944.

V34 410230 BMW 801F, forerunner of Fw 190A–9, armoured leading edges.

V35 0816 BMW 801TU, development aircraft for Fw 190A–8 and F–8.

V36 BMW 801F, probably not built.

V42 1083 BMW 801D–2, 2 × MG 151, Fw 190A–5/U2 prototype.

V45 7374 BMW 801TS with GM–1, Fw 190A–6/R4 prototype, extended wing tips.

V47 530115 BMW 801D–2 with GM–1, high aspect ratio wing, for extreme altitude tests.

V51 530765 BMW 801D–2, forerunner of A–6/R2, 2 × MG 131, 2 × MG 151 and 2 × MK 108 guns.

V52 170002 BMW 801D–2, Fw 190A–8 suicide conversion, to be fitted with 55mm MK 113A gun.

V53 170003 DU + UC, first Fw 190D–0 prototype, became V68.

V54 170024 Jumo 213A, second Fw 190D–2 prototype.

V55 170923 Jumo 213F, Fw 190D–11 prototype, converted A–8.

V56 170924 Jumo 213F, similar to V55, first flew August 31st, 1944.

V57 170926 Jumo 213F, similar to V55.

V58 170933 Jumo 213F, similar to V55.

V59 350156 Jumo 213F, similar to V55, crashed October 9th, 1944.

V60 350157 Jumo 213F, similar to V55 but no armament.

Typical of an ex-Luftwaffe airfield just after the war, this photo shows a large collection of Fw 190 variants including, in the foreground, a D(w/nr 176002), an F–8 and, being manhandled, a Ta 152H.

69

V61 350158 Jumo 213F, similar to V55, Junkers test aircraft.

V62 732053 Jumo 213F, Fw 190D–12 prototype.

V63 350165 Jumo 213, Fw 190D–12/R11 prototype.

V64 350166 Jumo 213, Fw 190D–12/R11 prototype.

V65 350167 Jumo 213, Fw 190D–12/R5 prototype.

V66 584002 BMW 801TS, Fw 190F–15 prototype.

V67 930516 BMW 801TS, Fw 190F–16 prototype.

V68 170003 Jumo 213E, rebuilt Fw 190 V53, Ta 152B–5 prototype.

V69 582072 X–4 guided missile tests, first flew August 11th, 1944.

V70 580029 X–4 missile tests, crashed August 25th, 1944.

V71 732054 Rebuilt Fw 190A–8, Fw 190D–12 prototype.

V72 170727 BMW 801TS, tested PKS directional control, completed August 5th, 1944.

V73 733705 Standard Fw 190A–8 airframe for test purposes.

V74 733713 Fitted with the SG 117 upward firing gun.

V75 582071 Modified Fw 190F–8 with the SG 113A anti-tank weapon.

V76 210040 Rebuilt Fw 190D–9 to D–14 standards.

V77 210040 Rebuilt Fw 190D–9 to D–14 standards.

V78 551103 Tested the AG 140 rocket launcher.

V79 581304 Tested the AG 140 rocket launcher.

V80 586600 Tested the AG 140 rocket launcher.

Fw 191

In July 1939, the technical department of the RLM issued the 'B Bomber' specification which called for a high performance aircraft with a pressurised cabin and remotely-controlled defensive armament, to be powered by two of the new 24-cylinder piston engines under development.

Several 24-cylinder engines were developed in Britain and Germany, but only one achieved some measure of success. This was the Napier Sabre unit which powered both the Hawker Typhoon and Tempest. The two most important German designs were the Daimler Benz DB 604 which comprised four banks of six cylinders arranged in an X formation, and the Junkers Jumo 222 which had four sets of six cylinders arranged radially around its crankcase. Neither engine was destined to be used operationally.

Initially four German manufacturers were asked to submit proposals for the 'B Bomber' specification, Arado developing the Ar 340, Dornier the Do 317, Focke-Wulf the Fw 191 and Junkers the Ju 288. The four designs were examined in July 1940, the Fw 191 and Ju 288 being favoured, the Ar 340 being abandoned and the Do 317 allocated low priority.

The task of producing detailed drawings for the Fw 191 was allocated to *Dipl Ing* E. Kosel who had previously worked on the Fw 189. The Fw 191 was a sleek shoulder-wing monoplane of all-metal stressed-skin construction with twin fins and rudders. The crew of four were grouped together in an extensively glazed nose and a fully retractable undercarriage was provided, the mainwheels folding backwards into the engine nacelles. The aircraft was designed around a pair of Jumo 222 engines (these showing consider-

The Fw 191 V1 is towed past a heavily camouflaged hanger by a tiny converted car. In the background is the tail of a Fw 200.

ably more promise than the DB 604) but, in the event the first two prototypes were fitted with 1,600hp BMW 801MA engines.

Early in 1942 the prototype, the Fw 191 V1, made its first flight with *Dipl Ing* Melhorn at the controls. It carried mock-ups of the proposed defensive armament which was to comprise a remotely-controlled chin turret containing two 7.9mm MG 81 machine-guns with a similar barbette in the rear of each engine nacelle. Provision was also to be made for a dorsal and ventral turret, each containing a 20mm MG 151/20 cannon and two 13mm MG 131 machine-guns. A bomb load of 4,000kg (8,820lb) could be carried in an internal bay and provision was made for two LT 950 torpedos beneath the wings.

With the 1,600hp BMW 801 engines the Fw 191 V1 was seriously underpowered, the machine weighing almost 45,000lb. Much of the excess weight resulted from an

RLM requirement that all systems should be actuated by electric motors. Focke-Wulf protested that this feature was entirely impractical under operational conditions, a single enemy bullet in the engine-driven generator being enough to put all systems out of action. The installation of the large number of electric motors led to the machine being nicknamed *Das fliegende Kraftwerk* (the flying powerstation).

Apart from difficulties associated with the failure of the electrically operated systems, the Fw 191 also encountered problems with the *Multhopp-Klappe*, an ingenious form of combined landing flap and dive brake developed by the aero-dynamics expert Hans Multhopp. When extended the flap presented severe flutter problems and pointed the need for urgent redesign.

After completing ten test flights, the Fw 191 V1 was joined by the similar V2,

but a total of only ten hours flying was logged before testing was halted. Eventually the RLM agreed to allow the electric motors to be replaced by hydraulic systems, this resulting in the abandoning of the V3, V4 and V5 and the modification of the V6 to the new standard. Apart from having hydraulically operated systems, the Fw 191 V6 also differed in being powered by a pair of early Jumo 222 engines which developed 2,200hp for take-off.

The Fw 191 V6 made its first flight in December 1942 with *Flugkapitän* Hans Sander at the controls. The Jumo 222 engine was far from satisfactory and it was realised that considerable development work had to be carried out before it could be used operationally.

Six further prototypes, designated Fw 191 V7, V8, V9, V10, V11 and V12 were proposed, powered either by BMW 801 Jumo 222, DB 606 or DB 610 engines.

The Fw 191 V1 takes shape at Bremen with an early production Fw 190 in the background.

The extensively glazed cockpit of the Fw 191 medium bomber. It is interesting to note that a panel on the starboard side carries the legend 'V13' but whether this refers to the prototype number is a matter of conjecture.

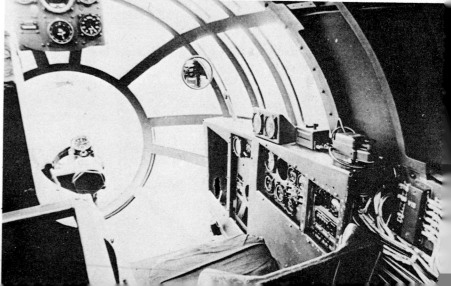

The pilot of the Fw 191 V1 runs up his engines prior to take-off.

The Fw 191 V1 with its bomb bay doors open.

The aircraft were forerunners of the proposed Fw 191B series which was to carry a total of six MG 151/20 cannon in chin, dorsal, ventral and tail barbettes, the engine nacelle positions being deleted.

In the event these aircraft were abandoned in favour of the Fw 191 V13 powered by two 2,700hp DB 606 engines and having manually-operated defensive armament. The Daimler Benz DB 606 and DB 610 engines comprised two DB 601 or DB 605 units coupled together to drive a single airscrew, and were considerably more advanced than the Jumo 222. Five further prototypes were projected, designated Fw 191 V14 to V18, but as far as is known, none were completed.

The final projected version of the aircraft was the Fw 191C powered by four separate engines and having manually-operated defensive armament. Power units proposed for the aircraft included the 1,340hp Jumo 211F, the 1,300hp DB 601E, the 1,475hp DB 605A and the 1,475hp DB 628. The Fw 191, like the advanced Fw 391 and Fw 491 projects, was abandoned at the end of 1943 contributing, with the Ju 288, to one of the saddest chapters in German aviation history.

Specification (Fw 191B)

POWERPLANTS	2 × 2,700hp Daimler Benz DB 606 in-lines
SPAN	26.00m (85ft 3½in)
LENGTH	19.63m (64ft 4¾in)
HEIGHT	5.60m (18ft 4½in)
WEIGHT EMPTY	16,300kg (35,942lb)
WEIGHT LOADED	23,600kg (52,038lb)
MAX SPEED	600km/h (373mph)
SERVICE CEILING	8,500m (27,880ft)
NORMAL RANGE	3,850km (2,390 miles)

Fw 200 Condor

By the spring of 1936, Lufthansa were becoming increasingly worried by the introduction of the American DC–2 into KLM service and the threat of the further improved DC–3. In order to keep Germany in the forefront of airliner development, Focke-Wulf's technical director, Kurt Tank, began preliminary work on a new transport, the first and only four-engined aircraft built by the company.

Tank's proposals were eventually put before two directors of Lufthansa, Dr Stüssel and *Freiherr* Karl August von Gablenz on July 16th, 1936. The Focke-Wulf designer had such confidence in his company's abilities that he promised that the aircraft would be ready to make its first flight in under a year—even betting a case of champagne on the result.

After four weeks intensive work, the first detailed drawings were produced for the aircraft. It was to be an all-metal low-wing monoplane of high aspect ratio powered by four radial engines. Accommodation was to be provided for nine in a forward smoking compartment, and 16–17 passengers in a larger cabin aft. A feature of the type was the specially engineered retractable undercarriage, designed to enable the slipstream to assist in lowering it should the normal retraction mechanism fail.

The airliner was named *Condor* by Tank, and such was its prestige value that the RLM allocated the special type number '200'—completely out of sequence with other Focke-Wulf designs. Work commenced on three prototypes in the autumn of 1936, and on July 27th, 1937 one of

these, the initially unmarked Fw 200 V1, made its first flight. Despite the record time in which the aircraft was completed, it was 11 days over the year specified, and Tank lost his bet. The blow was somewhat softened when Gablenz sent him a case of champagne in return to congratulate him on his magnificent feat in producing the aircraft in such a short time.

Following initial trials, the Fw 200 V1 (w/nr 2000) was given the registration D–AERE and named *Saarland*. It was powered by four 875hp Pratt and Whitney Hornet SIE–G radials and proved to have excellent flight characteristics. Two further prototypes followed, both being powered by four 820hp BMW 132G–1 nine-cylinder radials. These were the Fw 200 V2 (w/nr 2484) D–AETA *Westfalen* and the V3, D–2600 *Immelmann III* which was used as a personal transport by Adolf Hitler.

Apart from the Fw 200 V2, four of a

batch of nine Fw 200A–0s were delivered to Lufthansa. These were the A–01 (w/nr 2893) D–ADHR *Saarland*, the A–03 (w/nr 2895) D–AMHC *Nordmark*, the A–06 (w/nr 2994) D–ARHW *Friesland* and the A–09 D–AXFO *Pommern*. These aircraft were also known respectively as the Fw 200 V4, V5, V7 and V9. A fifth *Condor*, the A–04 or V6, D–ACVH *Grenzmark* was delivered to the Luftwaffe for use as a staff aircraft, flying Ribbentrop to meet Stalin in Moscow in 1939.

On June 27th, 1938, the Fw 200A–01 with Tank and Hans Sander taking turns at the controls, made a long-distance flight from Berlin to Cairo via Salonica. This was followed by a number of record breaking flights by the first *Condor* now redesignated Fw 200S–1 and registered D–ACON *Brandenburg*. On August 10th, 1938 this aircraft, with Lufthansa pilot Alfred Henke at the controls, flew non-stop

The Fw 200 V1 in its original form before the markings D–AERE were applied.

from Berlin to New York in 24hr, 56min and 12sec. Three days later the aircraft completed the return flight in 19hr, 55min and 1sec. A third flight was made on November 28th, 1938 when D-ACON flew from Berlin to Tokyo via Basra, Karachi and Hanoi in a time of 46hr, 18min and 19sec. Perhaps strangely in these days of fast jet travel, these three records still stand.

Of the initial batch of nine Fw 200As, the remaining four aircraft were delivered to foreign airlines. The A-02 (w/nr 2894) OY-DAM *Dania* and the A-05 (w/nr 2993) OY-DEM *Jutlandia* were delivered to the Danish airline DDL and the A-07 (w/nr 2995) initially D-ASBK and later PP-CBJ *Arumani* and the A-08 (w/nr 2996) PP-CBI *Abaitara* were delivered to Lufthansa's Brazilian affiliate Syndicato Condor Ltd.

Towards the end of 1938 the first of a small series of Fw 200B transports were delivered. These differed in having increased all-up weight and some structural strengthening. Only one Fw 200B-1, D-ASBR *Holstein* was built, this being powered by four 850hp BMW 132Dc radials.

A batch of five Fw 200B-2s, powered by 830hp BMW 132H-1 engines, was ordered by the Japanese airline, Dai Nippon KK, and two further machines were to be built for the Finnish company, Aero OY. In the event none of these aircraft were delivered before the beginning of the war, the three machines completed passing to Lufthansa as D-ABOD *Kurmark*, D-ASHH *Hessen* and D-AMHL *Pommern* (the original *Pommern* having been destroyed in a crash).

Early in April 1940 the four Fw 200Bs

The first Condor *after receiving the registration D-AERE but prior to delivery to Lufthansa.*

One of a small batch of Fw 200A-Os, the ninth Condor *was named* Pommern *and served for a short period with Lufthansa.*

were transferred from Lufthansa to KGrzbV 105 at Kiel-Holtenau to operate in support of the forthcoming invasion of Norway. After the successful completion of the campaign, two aircraft (D-ABOD and D-ASHH were returned to Lufthansa to operate alongside D-ADHR and D-AMHC. In 1941 two of these machines, D-ADHR and D-ABOD were lost, followed by D-AMHC in 1943. The remaining aircraft, D-ASHH, has the distinction of making Lufthansa's last scheduled service of the war on April 14th, 1945 when it flew from Barcelona to Berlin. The return flight, seven days later, ended in disaster when the aircraft crashed in Bavaria.

As previously mentioned, the Japanese airline, Dai Nippon KK had ordered five Fw 200B-2 transports but these failed to be delivered. At the same time, the Japanese Navy placed an order for a long-range maritime reconnaissance version of the *Condor*. This was eventually produced as the Fw 200 V10, the machine having considerably increased fuel tankage and provision for a 7.9mm MG 15 machine-gun in a dorsal position and a similar weapon in a short ventral gondola.

When war was declared in September 1939, Germany found herself without a long-range anti-shipping aircraft. The Heinkel He 177 which was designed to fulfil this rôle had yet to fly, and the Luftwaffe was forced to a makeshift. Therefore Focke-Wulf were asked to produce a long-range maritime reconnaissance and anti-shipping development of the *Condor* drawing on their previous experience with the Fw 200 V10.

A batch of ten aircraft were ordered by the RLM in September 1939 under the designation Fw 200C-0. The variant was basically a development of the Fw 200B-2 with long-chord engine cowlings, twin mainwheels and three-bladed variable pitch airscrews. The first Fw 200C-0 (w/nr 021) D-ASVX *Thüringen* was unarmed and intended for delivery to Lufthansa, but in the event it, and the next three aircraft, were diverted to the Luftwaffe transport unit KGrzbV 105 for operations in the Norwegian campaign.

The remaining six aircraft (Fw 200C-05 to C-010) were fitted with defensive armament. A 7.9mm MG 15 machine-gun was carried in a forward dorsal turret, a similar weapon was positioned in the rear of an after dorsal turret, and a third gun was mounted below the fuselage, firing through a ventral hatch. The first production model, the Fw 200C-1 differed in having a long ventral gondola which

Two Condors, *O Y–DAM* Dania *and* O Y–DEM Jutlandia, *were operated by Danish Air Lines.*

For a series of long-distance flights undertaken in 1938, the Fw 200 V1 was re-registered D–ACON and named Brandenburg.

One of a small batch of Fw 200Bs which saw service with KGrzbV 105 during the Norwegian campaign.

mounted a forward-firing 20mm MG FF cannon with a MG 15 machine-gun firing aft. Both aircraft had provision for four 250kg (550lb) bombs, although the C–1 could carry a 250kg concrete bomb in its ventral gondola for aiming purposes. The Fw 200C–2 was similar to the C–1, but introduced modified rear engine nacelles and more streamlined bomb racks.

The fuselage of the Fw 200C was an all-metal semi-monocoque structure with provision for a crew of five. This normally comprised a pilot, co-pilot, navigator/radio operator/bomb aimer/gunner, engineer/gunner and rear dorsal gunner. The wing was a two spar structure built of metal, with metal covering forward of the rear spar and fabric aft. Two-piece ailerons and split flaps were provided and the specially designed retractable undercarriage developed for the original airliner variant was retained. The complete tail assembly was an all-metal stressed-skin structure.

On October 1st, 1939, a special long-range reconnaissance unit was formed at Bremen to operate the six armed Fw 200C–0s then under construction. This unit, the *Fernaufklärungstaffel*, was placed under the command of *Oberstlt* Edgar Petersen, eventually being redesignated as 1./KG 40 during the spring of 1940. Early operations by the squadron included armed reconnaissance flights over the North Sea during **the** German invasion of Norway and **Denmark**, including a strike against British ships in the Harstadt-Namsos area.

The squadron was withdrawn from operations in late June 1940, redesignated as I.*Gruppe*/KG 40 and re-equipped with the Fw 200C–1. Early in July, the group became operational at Bordeaux-Merignac, the French airfield becoming the unit's main base. Co-operating closely with the naval command *Marine Gruppe West* at Lorient, the *Condors* of I./KG 40 usually flew search operations over the Bay of Biscay, then followed a wide arc to the west of Ireland, finally landing at Stavanger-Sola or Trondheim-Vaernes in Norway.

A Ju 88 equipped staff flight was added to KG 40 early in August, and at the end of the month four experimental night bombing attacks were made by the group's Fw 200s on the Liverpool–Birkenhead area. Tests were also made to investigate the suitability of the *Condor* as a minelayer. Carrying two huge 1,000kg (2,200lb) mines beneath the wings the machine proved completely unwieldy, and after heavy losses the experiments were abandoned. During August and September 1940, I./KG 40 claimed the destruction of 90,000 tons of Allied shipping, but the most spectacular success came on October 26th, 1940 when *Oblt* Bernhard Jope, flying his first operational mission, bombed the 42,000-ton liner *Empress of Britain*. Taken in tow off Donegal Bay, the liner was sunk two days later by the German submarine U–32.

Towards the end of 1940, rarely more than eight *Condors* were available to I./KG 40 at one time. The main trouble was the speed with which the aircraft had been adapted from a commercial airliner. The *Condor* was not intended for continuous operational flying, sometimes accompanied by violent evasive manoeuvres at low altitudes, and frequently the rear spar failed and the fuselage aft of the wing trailing edge cracked.

In an attempt to solve the problems associated with the weak structure of the *Condor*, the Fw 200C-3 was introduced during the summer of 1941. The new variant was considerably structurally strengthened and to offset the increased weight imposed by the modifications, the BMW 132H engines were replaced by Bramo 323R-2 radials which delivered 1,200hp for take-off. Armament was similar to that of the Fw 200C-1, but the forward gun position was replaced by a Fw 19 hydraulically operated gun turret.

The Fw 200C-3/U1 had the Fw 19 barbette replaced by the larger HDL 151 turret which mounted a 15mm MG 151 cannon and the faster-firing 20mm MG 151/20 gun was substituted for the older MG FF weapon in the ventral position. The Fw 200C-3/U2 reverted to the Fw 19 turret, but carried the *Lotfe* 7D computer bomb sight in the ventral position. In order to accommodate this feature, the MG 151/20 weapon was replaced by a 13mm MG 131 machine-gun. The Fw 200C-3/U3 carried a MG 131 gun in an EDL 131 forward turret and a similar weapon in the rear dorsal station and the C-3/U4 had an extra gunner and two MG 131 guns firing through beam positions.

An unusual in-flight photo of one of Kampfgeschwader *40's Condors.*

During the summer of 1942, the Fw 200C-3 was replaced by the C-4 on the production lines. This variant carried a 15mm MG 151 cannon in a HDL 151 forward dorsal turret, a MG 131 or MG 151/20 weapon in the ventral position, and MG 15 machine-guns at all other stations. Apart from its armament, the Fw 200C-4 differed mainly in carrying FuG 200 *Hohentwiel* search radar, a large 'toasting fork' aerial array being attached to the nose of the aircraft.

Late in January 1941, a third group was added to KG 40, although because of the shortage of Fw 200s, it was equipped initially with the He 111. During 1941 only 58 *Condors* were completed, the Bremen production line suffering heavily from Allied bombing, necessitating the transference of some work to the Blohm und Voss plant in Hamburg, and the establishment of a second assembly line at Cottbus. The shortage of *Condors* was so acute that at one stage a crew from KG 40 was sent to collect each new aircraft as it came off the production line.

Despite difficulties in aircraft replacement, 15 ships totalling 63,000 tons were sunk by I./KG 40 in January 1941, followed by 22 vessels totalling 84,500 tons in February. Between August 1st, 1940 and February 9th, 1941 no less than 85 ships with a combined tonnage of 363,000 were sunk by the group. Several notable individual achievements with the Fw 200 occurred about this time. On January 16th, *Hptm* Verlohr, leader of 1./KG 40, sank two ships totalling 10,857 tons and in February, *Hptm* Fritz Fliegel, commander of 2./KG 40, led an attack on Iceland.

The middle of 1941 saw the introduction of a considerable number of *Condor* countermeasures aboard British ships. Apart from conventional 20mm anti-aircraft weapons and light machine-guns, several ingenious devices were produced. These included a rocket which launched a wire cable into the path of the oncoming aircraft and a steam pressure device which projected a hand grenade into the air. Far more impressive however were the catapult merchant ships operated by the Royal Navy. These were conventional merchant ships modified to launch a Hawker Hurricane fighter with the aid of a catapult from the specially modified foredeck of the vessel. The main drawback to the scheme was that the pilot, after attacking, had to ditch his aircraft in the sea and hope to be rescued by escort vessels.

The first success by a catapult merchant ship came on August 3rd, 1941 when Lt R. W. H. Everett of No 804 Squadron from HMS *Maplin* shot down a Fw 200 from I./KG 40. In all, about 50 merchant ships were fitted with catapults, but many were sunk by German U-boats and failed to launch their aircraft. The real solution to the menace of the *Condor* came with the introduction of the escort carrier from September 1941.

By the autumn of 1941 *Condor* losses had started to rise alarmingly, and pilots began to restrict their attacks to a hastily executed bombing run from higher altitudes. The introduction of the *Lotfe* 7D computer bomb-sight mentioned earlier enabled the *Condor* to make accurate attacks from over 10,000ft, but even there the machine was not immune from the operations of British fighters.

In October 1941, *Gen-Maj* Martin Harlinghausen, leader of the anti-shipping command, *Fliegerführer Atlantik* was wounded during an attack on a convoy escort in the Bristol Channel. Although a deputy was appointed, it was not until early 1942 that another officer was allowed to take his place. The third *Gruppe* of KG 40, operating from Bordeaux-Merignac, received its first *Condors* at this time.

A notable engagement took place on December 16th, 1941 when a *Condor* from KG 40 reported the position of a homeward bound convoy from Gibraltar and radioed the information to waiting German U-boats. Six submarines attacked the convoy, coded HG 76, but the Condors suffered heavily from Wildcat fighters from the escort carrier HMS *Audacity*.

Early in 1942, I./KG 40 was transferred to Trondheim-Vaernes in Norway, and in May, *Oberst* Pasewaldt took over from Petersen as commander of the Geschwader. Earlier, in March and April 1942, three Allied convoys, PQ 13, 14 and 15 sailed through Arctic waters to Archangel and Murmansk in northern Russia. Following reconnaissance reports by *Condors* from I./KG 40, all three convoys were attacked by He 111s from KG 26 and Ju 88s from KG 30 but little damage was done. On May 25th, convoy PQ 16 comprising 34 ships sailed from Iceland. Sighting reports from I./KG 40 were relayed to *Luftflotte* 5 headquarters at Banak and aircraft from KG 26, KG 30, coastal reconnaissance groups 406, 706 and 906 and St.G 5 attacked the convoy, sinking seven ships and severely damaging many more.

The next convoy, PQ 17 with 34 ships, set out from Hvalfjord in Iceland on June 27th, 1942. It was sighted on July 1st by a Fw 200 of 3./KG 40 and continuously shadowed. The first concentrated attacks by aircraft from KG 26 and KG 30 were made on July 4th and after these, the convoy scattered. From then on the Luftwaffe attempted to seek out each ship

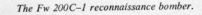

The Fw 200C-1 reconnaissance bomber.

and destroy it separately, and in the event only 11 vessels reached port.

Following the Allied breakthrough at El Alamein in November 1942, 9./KG 40 was transferred from Bordeaux to Lecce in southern Italy to fly transport operations in support of Rommel's troops. Together with Ju 52/3ms, the Fw 200s succeeded in transporting 250 tons of petrol a day. On January 1st, 1943 7. and 8./KG 40 bombed Casablanca on the initiative of the commander of III.*Gruppe*, dropping 550lb bombs on the city. Several *Condors* suffered damage from anti-aircraft fire, two machines having to force-land in Spain. One of these was written off, but the other (F8 + JR, w/nr 0166) was repaired and taken over by the Spanish airline Iberia. On landing back at Bordeaux, the commander of III./KG 40 was severely reprimanded for his unofficial action.

Late in 1942, a few *Condors* were delivered to other Luftwaffe units, although KG 40 remained the major operator of the type. Other units to fly the *Condor* included 1.(F)/120, Norway, 1.(F)/122 at Sardinia and II./KG 100 at Kalamaki, Greece.

With the approaching obsolescence of the *Condor*, the aircraft was switched more and more to transport operations. Two specialised transport variants had been built in 1942, the first of which, the Fw 200C-4/U1 (w/nr 137) could carry 11 passengers. Armament included a Fw 19 turret in the forward dorsal position and a Fw 20 in the after position, both carrying a single MG 15 machine-gun. The Fw 200C-4/U2 (w/nr 138) was similar to the U1 but carried 14 seats and the C-4/U3 was a reconnaissance-bomber with a Fw 19 turret in place of the HDL 151 position of the standard variant.

By the end of 1942 the plight of the surrounded VI *Armee* at Stalingrad was becoming serious. In a desperate attempt to supply the garrison, 18 *Condors* from 1. and 3./KG 40 were transferred from Bordeaux to Stalino, some 300 miles from the city. Redesignated as KGrzbV 200, the unit was put under the command of *Maj* Hans Jürgen Williers, and made its first operation on January 9th, 1943. Seven *Condors* led by *Oblt* Franz Schulte-Vogelheim landed at Stalingrad's Pitomnik airfield with 36 tons of supplies. The aircraft returned to Stalino with 156 wounded. Subsequent operations in the harsh Russian winter resulted in severe losses, and on January 18th the unit was transferred to Zaparozhe, making a further 41 flights over Stalingrad and 35 over the Crimea.

In February 1943 the remnants of KGrzbV 200 were withdrawn to Berlin-Staaken where they were amalgamated to form 8./KG 40. The unit was then transferred to Bordeaux-Merignac, joining 7. and 9.*Staffeln* to complete the *Gruppe*. At this time only the *Geschwader Stab*, 2.*Staffel* and III./KG 40 were equipped with the Fw 200C-4, the squadrons concentrating on anti-shipping attacks far out into the Atlantic. KG 40 usually acted

Many of the early operational Condors *bore the names of stars. This aircraft, bearing the famous 'world in a ring' insignia of KG 40, was named* Wega.

Three Fw 200Cs, a Ju 52/3m and a Ju 352 possibly of the Führer Kurier Staffel, *Hitler's personal transport squadron. The aircraft numbered '5' was used by Heinrich Himmler.*

on the sighting reports provided by the Ju 290s of FAGr 5 based at Mont de Marsan. The Ju 290* was, like the *Condor*, a development of a civil airliner.

Reports were received from Algeciras in Spain when Allied convoys left Gibraltar and aircraft from FAGr 5 would be sent out to attack the convoy, the aircraft making full use of their *Hohentwiel* search radar. The *Condor* was now forbidden to attack at altitudes of less than 9,000ft because of the increased efficiency of the anti-aircraft guns carried by Allied vessels.

A Fw 200 had been specially modified late in 1942 as a launching vehicle for the Fieseler Fi 103 flying bomb (later to become known as the V-1). In December, Gerhard Fieseler released the first Fi 103 over Peenemünde, the initial catapult launching taking place a month later.

During the summer of 1943 several Fw 200C-3/U1 and U2s were modified to carry two Henschel 293A rocket-propelled guided bombs underwing. The variant was designated Fw 200C-6 and entered service with III./KG 40 in November 1943. The Henschel Hs 293, which was designed early in 1940 by Prof Herbert Wagner, was powered by a 1,300lb thrust Walter HWK 507 rocket engine which gave it a final speed of between 270 and 560mph depending on height of launching and angle of descent. The main production model, the Hs 293A, utilised radio control, later variants used wire and television guidance techniques.

The Fw 200C-6 was merely a stop-gap pending the introduction of the purpose-built C-8. This variant had a Henschel Hs 293A missile mounted beneath each

* See *Junkers—An Aircraft Album*, page 114.

Top left: *Line-up of four Fw 200C–4s seen from beneath the wing of a fifth aircraft.*

Bottom left: *The Fw 200C–4 fitted with FuG 200 Hohentwiel search radar.*

outboard engine nacelle, and was ïtted with *Hohentwiel* search radar and a ¹ mm cannon in a HDL 151 turret in the for ard dorsal position. Radio equipment was supplemented by a FuG 203b *Kehl* transmitter which operated in conjunction with the FuG 230b *Strassburg* receiver mounted in the Hs 293.

The first operational mission by an Hs 293-carrying Fw 200 was made on December 28th, 1943 when one of four *Condors* on an anti-shipping strike was so equipped. The Hs 293-carrying machine encountered a patrolling Coastal Command Sunderland flying boat and was forced to ditch in the sea without having a chance to launch its missiles. A few further operations were flown by Hs 293-carrying *Condors*, but the main missile launching operations were carried out by I./KG 40 with He 177s and II. and III./KG 100 with Do 217s.

By the late spring of 1944, *Condor* operations had declined to almost nothing and finally, on June 7th, the remaining Fw 200 *Staffeln* were transferred from Bordeaux to Norway and Germany. Lack of fuel and poor serviceability resulted in few further operational flights being undertaken. On August 26th, 1944, *Oblt* Bieberger, Technical Officer of I./KG 40 was killed while flying from France to Germany and shortly afterwards the complete *Geschwader* was disbanded.

After the dissolution of KG 40, 8.*Staffel* was re-designated as *Transport Flieger Staffel Condor* and began supply operations from Norwegian bases in October 1944. Three Fw 200s passed to *Transportstaffel 5* in December and in the late spring of 1945 a second squadron was formed with the *Condor* designated *Transportstaffel 200* and based at Horschii

Several *Condc* also equipped the *Führer Kurier alfel* commanded by Hitler's personal Δt Heinz Baur. A few of these aircraft, including those of both Hitler and Himmler, had specially armoured seats incorporating a parachute. A quick-release hatch was provided to allow the special passenger to bale out in case of attack. Himmler's aircraft was captured by the Allies after the war and flown to Farnborough.

Specification (Fw 200 V6)

POWERPLANTS	4 × 720hp BMW 132L radials
SPAN	33.00m (108ft 3¼in)
LENGTH	23.85m (76ft 11½in)
HEIGHT	6.00m (19ft 8¼in)
WEIGHT EMPTY	9,800kg (21,605lb)
WEIGHT LOADED	14,600kg (31,987lb)
CRUISING SPEED	325km/h (202mph)
SERVICE CEILING	6,700m (21,981ft)
NORMAL RANGE	1,250km (776 miles)

(Fw 200C-3)

POWERPLANTS	4 × 1,200hp Bramo 323R radials
SPAN	32.84m (107ft 9½in)
LENGTH	23.85m (76ft 11½in)
HEIGHT	6.30m (20ft 8in)
WEIGHT EMPTY	12,950kg (28,554lb)
WEIGHT MAX	22,700kg (50,053lb)
MAX SPEED	360km/h (224mph)
SERVICE CEILING	6,000m (19,686ft)
NORMAL RANGE	3,560km (2,211 miles)

Ta 152 and Ta 153

Perhaps the one chance of halting or at least easing the daylight bombing offensive by the USAAF on the German homeland was the massive production of the radically new jet fighters. The foresightedness of such men as Ernst Heinkel and Willy Messerschmitt had ensured that Germany was well ahead in the development of jet aircraft, but it was an advantage that her leaders were unwilling to exploit. Many thought that even a temporary interruption of existing Bf 109 and Fw 190 production would be disastrous, and pressed the German aircraft industry to develop improved versions of these excellent, if then uninspiring machines to avoid any such disruption.

The most demanding need was to improve the high altitude capabilities of both the Bf 109 and Fw 190. Tank's proposals centred around developments of the D-series airframe under the designations Fw 190Ra-2, Ra-3 and Ra-4. The Ra-2 and Ra-3 were similar with Jumo 213E engines and both MW-50 and GM-1 injection. A lengthened fuselage and larger tail surface area was chosen for both machines, the Ra-3 differing in having increased wing span.

The Fw 190Ra-4 was to be powered by a Daimler Benz DB 603 engine and employ a completely new wing. Development of the variant continued under the designation Ta 153, the wing developed for the type having slightly increased span and area. In the event only one development aircraft for the Ta 153 was completed, the Fw 190 V32/U1 which was fitted with the new wing.

Development of the Fw 190Ra-2 and Ra-3 projects commenced under the respective designations Ta 152B ('B' for *Begleitjäger* or escort fighter) and Ta 152H ('H' for *Höhenjäger* or high altitude fighter). The first prototype was the Ta 152 V1 (w/nr 110001) which was completed at

The Fw 190 V30/U1 which served as a prototype for the Ta 152H-O but crashed on August 13th, 1944.

Langenhagen in June 1944. This was followed by the Fw 190 V33/U1 which was fitted with the definitive wing intended for the Ta 152H–1. This wing had a span of 47ft 6¾in and incorporated five fuel tanks plus a container for MW–50 methanol-water injection.

The Ta 152 V2 (w/nr 110002) was followed by the Fw 190 V30/U1 which was basically a Fw 190D–9 airframe fitted with the H–0 long-span wing. Three further Ta 152 prototypes were joined, in September 1944, by the Fw 190 V29/U1 which was fitted with a 2,060hp Jumo 213F engine and cabin pressurization. Three other Fw 190 prototypes joined the Ta 152 programme in October and November, the V18/U2, V20/U1 and V32/U1, the latter having been fitted with the wing from the partially completed Ta 152 V25. The aircraft was later re-engined with the Jumo 213E and fitted with the ultra fast-firing MG 213C cannon under the designation Fw 190 V32/U2.

In October 1944 the first of a batch of 20 pre-production Ta 152H–0s (w/nrs 150001 to 150020) left Focke-Wulf's Cottbus assembly line, being delivered to *Erprobungskommando* 152 at Rechlin under *Hptm* Bruno Stolle. The first Ta 152H–1 production aircraft followed at the end of November, the variant being powered by a 1,750hp Jumo 213E engine and carrying an armament of one engine-mounted 30mm MK 108 with two 20mm MG 151/20 cannon in the wing roots.

Top right: Close-up of the nose of the Fw 190 V30/U1.

Bottom right: The high aspect ratio wing of the Ta 152H is clearly visible in this photo.

Several *Rüstsätze* conversion packs were designed for the Ta 152H–0 and H–1 including the R11, which incorporated FuG 125 blind landing equipment and the LGW-Siemens K 23 autopilot, the R21, which introduced MW–50 injection in place of GM–1, and the R31 which had an extra 61 Imp gallon fuel tank aft of the cockpit. The projected Ta 152H–2 with improved radio equipment and the Ta 152H–10 fighter-reconnaissance aircraft were not completed. The Ta 152H was also proposed with the 2,500hp Jumo 222 engine, but this unit was abandoned early in 1945.

The projected Ta 152B–1 and B–2 (to be powered by Jumo 213 or DB 603 'power eggs') and the Ta 152B–3 ground-attack aircraft were abandoned in favour of the B–4. This variant was intended to carry an armament of one engine-mounted 30mm cannon and four wing guns, but was in turn replaced by the Ta 152B–5. This was to be powered by a Jumo 213E engine and carry three 30mm cannon. Four proto-types were completed, the Fw 190 V68 and the Ta 152 V19, V20 and V21.

The last three aircraft were all equipped with FuG 125 radio equipment and the K 23 autopilot under the designation Ta 152B–5/R11. No production of the Ta 152B was undertaken before the end of the war mainly because of the high

Top left: *The Focke-Wulf Ta 152 V3 (w/nr 110003), forerunner of the H–0.*

Bottom left: *An early production Ta 152H–0 (w/nr 150005) mounted on a compass swinging platform.*

priority allocated to the C-series. The final projected variant was the Ta 152B–7 to be powered by the 2,240hp Jumo 213J engine.

A specialised reconnaissance version of the fighter was also developed under the designations Ta 152E–1 and E–2. These machines were similar to the B–5, carrying an armament of one 30mm MK 108 and two 20mm MG 151/20 cannon plus a vertically-mounted Rb 75/30 camera. The Ta 152E–2 differed from the first production machine in having GM–1 injection. Two prototypes of the variant were proposed, the Ta 152 V9 and V14, but both were abandoned in November 1944 before completion.

At an early stage in the development of the Ta 152, Tank had requested that he be allowed to install the Daimler Benz DB 603 engine in the aircraft. Although possessing a similar take-off performance to the Jumo 213, the DB 603 developed much increased power at altitude. Eventually the RLM agreed to Tank's request and development of a DB 603 powered fighter was instituted under the designation Ta 152C.

In October 1944 the Fw 190 V21 was fitted with a 1,750hp DB 603B engine under the designation V21/U1. The aircraft was rebuilt a second time with a 2,100hp DB 603LA engine and a centrally-mounted 30mm MK 108 cannon. Now designated Fw 190 V21/U2, the machine rejoined the

Top right: The Focke-Wulf Ta 152H high altitude fighter.

Bottom right: One Ta 152H–1 was taken to America after the war and given the field evaluation number FE 112.

test programme on November 19th, 1944. The first true C-series prototypes were the Ta 152 V6, V7 and V8, the former being completed on December 3rd. The Ta 152 V7 was fitted with FuG 125 radio equipment under the alternative designation Ta 152C–0/R11 and the V8 introduced the experimental EZ 42 computer gunsight.

The Ta 152 V13 and V15 were intended as the forerunners of the proposed Ta 152C–1 but were abandoned at an early stage. The Ta 152C–1 was to carry an armament of an engine-mounted 30mm MK 108 cannon with two 20mm MG 151/20 weapons above the engine and two similar guns in the wings. The V16 and V17, intended as prototypes of the Ta 152C–2 with improved radio, eventually flew in April 1945. The Ta 152C–3 was a development of the C–1 in which the 30mm MK 108 cannon was replaced by the longer range MK 103 of similar calibre. Two prototypes were converted from H–0 airframes under the designations Ta 152 V27 and V28, these flying in March and April 1945.

Several advanced versions of the aircraft were projected including the Ta 152C–4, with provision for FuG 15 radio and WGr 21 rocket tubes, and the C–11/R11 reconnaissance fighter with an Rb 75/30 camera. The Ta 152S–1 was a proposed two-seat trainer variant based on the Fw 190A–8/U1.

Between November 1944 and April 1945 about 190 Ta 152H–1 fighters were delivered from the Cottbus assembly line. With a maximum speed of 472mph, the Ta 152 possessed an impressive performance. On one notable occasion late in 1944, Tank himself was flying a Ta 152H from Langenhagen to Cottbus when he was intercepted by a section of USAAF Mustangs. Tank quickly operated the MW–50 injection control, and left the American fighters far behind. The Ta 152H was delivered in small numbers to several Luftwaffe units, the most important of which was JG 301 under *Oberstlt* Aufhammer, protecting Me 262 jet fighter bases.

Specification (Ta 152H–1)

POWERPLANT	1 × 1,750hp (2,050hp with MW–50) Jumo 213E–1 in-line
SPAN	14.50m (47ft 6¾in)
LENGTH	10.80m (35ft 5½in)
HEIGHT	4.00m (13ft 1½in)
WEIGHT EMPTY	3,920kg (8,643lb)
WEIGHT LOADED	4,750kg (10,472lb)
MAX SPEED*	760km/h (472mph)
SERVICE CEILING	14,800m (48,560ft)
NORMAL RANGE	1,200km (745 miles)

* The speed quoted is that attainable with the advantage of MW–50 injection.

Ta 152 Prototypes

V1 110001 First Ta 152H–0 prototype, Jumo 213E engine, flew in June 1944 at Langenhagen.

V2 110002 Second Ta 152H–0 prototype, Jumo 213E engine, flew in July 1944 at Langenhagen.

V3 110003 Third Ta 152H–0 prototype, Jumo 213E engine.

V4 110004 Fourth Ta 152H–0 prototype, Jumo 213E engine.

V5 110005 Fifth Ta 152H–0 prototype, Jumo 213E engine.

V6 110006 First true Ta 152C–0 prototype, DB 603LA engine, flew February 28th, 1945 at Langenhagen.

V7 110007 Ta 152C–0/R11 prototype, DB 603L engine, first flew March 10th, 1945, later to be fitted with ETC 504 weapon racks as forerunner of the proposed Ta 152C–1/R14.

V8 110008 Ta 152C prototype, DB 603L

The Ta 152 V7, prototype for the Ta 152C–0/R11 powered by a DB 603L engine.

engine, EZ 42 computer gunsight, first flew 1945.

V9 110009 Ta 152E-1 reconnaissance fighter prototype, shelved November 1944.

V13 110013 Ta 152C-1 prototype, abandoned.

V14 110014 Ta 152E-1 reconnaissance fighter prototype, shelved November 1944.

V15 110015 Ta 152C-1 prototype, abandoned.

V16 110016 Ta 152C-2 prototype, DB 603L engine, first flown April 1945.

V17 110017 Ta 152C-2 prototype, DB 603L engine, first flown April 1945.

V18 110018 Ta 152C-3/R11 prototype, abandoned late 1944.

V19 110019 Ta 152B-5 prototype, Jumo 213E engine, flown March 1945.

V20 110020 Ta 152B-5 prototype, Jumo 213 engine.

V21 110021 Ta 152B-5 prototype, Jumo 213 engine.

V22 110022 Intended as prototype of the Ta 152C-4 to be completed February/March 1945, abandoned.

V23 110023 As Ta 152 V22.

V24 110024 As Ta 152 V22.

V25 110025 Ta 152H-1 prototype, abandoned in 1944, wings fitted to Fw 190 V32/U1.

V26 110026 Ta 152H-1 prototype, first flew March 1945.

V27 150030 Converted Ta 152H-1 airframe, C-3 series prototype, first flew March 1945.

V28 150031 Converted Ta 152H-1 airframe, C-3 series prototype, first flew April 1945.

(No information is available on the Ta 152 V10, V11 and V12—respectively w/nrs 110010, 110011 and 110012).

Ta 154

The increasing RAF night bomber raids on the German homeland, culminating in the 1,000 aircraft attack on Cologne at the end of May 1942, led the German high command to consider at last the development of a specialised night fighter aircraft. Previously the Luftwaffe had been forced to make use of converted heavy fighters and medium bombers such as the Bf 110, Ju 88 and Do 17, for its newly established night fighter arm, but in August 1942 a specification was issued for the development of a purpose built machine.

Two companies were asked to work on the specification, Heinkel and Focke-Wulf. Heinkel had already designed the He 219, a fast bomber project which he considered could easily be adapted to meet the requirements of the specification, but Kurt Tank decided on an entirely new approach to the problem. His design was known initially as the Ta 211, this being the first time that the 'Ta' prefix had been used for a Focke-Wulf project.

By November 1942, Focke-Wulf had been allocated a new batch of type numbers from 152 to 154, and Tank decided to rechristen his design the Ta 154. The number '211' was subsequently allocated to a development of the He 219 designed by Dr Hütter. The task of producing detailed drawings for the Ta 154 was allocated to *Dipl Ing* Ernst Nipp who produced a neat shoulder wing design with twin underslung engines. It was unusual for aircraft of the time in being built almost entirely of wood. Only the control surfaces, part of the forward fuselage and the engine cowlings were constructed of duralumin.

After a remarkably short development period, the Ta 154 V1 (w/nr 0001) made its first flight from Langenhagen on July 1st, 1943. The aircraft had a crew of two seated in tandem, featured a fully retract-

The Fw 190 V32/U1 (w/nr 0057) which tested the wing intended for the Ta 153.

able nosewheel undercarriage and was powered by a pair of Jumo 211R engines which developed 1,350hp for take-off. Early trials with *Flugkapitän* Hans Sander at the controls showed that a speed of 435mph was attainable.

The Ta 154 V2 (w/nr 0002) was similar to the first aircraft apart from having FuG 212 *Lichtenstein* C–1 radar equipment with a four-prong antenna mounted in the nose. The V3, which made its first flight on November 25th, 1943, differed in being powered by a pair of Jumo 213E engines which produced 1,750hp for take-off and carried an armament of a 20mm MG 151/20 and a 30mm MK 108 cannon on either side of the fuselage.

Initial testing proved quite satisfactory, although the installation of radar equipment, armour protection and armament reduced the aircraft's maximum speed to 404mph. Nevertheless, the RLM placed an order for 250 Ta 154A–1 production aircraft, the V3 or A–03/U1 acting as production prototype. Consideration was also given to the development of the Ta 154A–2 single-seat day fighter, the A–3 two-seat day fighter and the A–4 two-seat night fighter projects.

Four other prototypes were completed at Langenhagen, the Ta 154 V4, V5, V6 and V7 (w/nrs 0004 to 0007). These aircraft were first flown respectively on January 19th, February 23rd and early and late

Top left: *The Ta 154 V1 prepares for take-off from Hannover-Langenhagen airfield during the summer of 1943.*

Bottom left: *The Ta 154 V1 after the application of camouflage.*

March 1944. Construction of the remaining eight prototypes from the original order was switched to the Focke-Wulf plant at Erfurt. The last of these was the Ta 154 V15 which made its first flight on June 30th, 1944. At least seven additional prototypes (V16 to V22) were ordered but probably not built. These were to be powered by 1,776hp Jumo 213A engines and carry, like the V15, FuG 220 *Lichtenstein* SN-2 radar.

The first two production aircraft (w/nrs 320001 and 320002) were completed at Erfurt in May and June 1944. On June 28th, the wing of the second aircraft disintegrated in flight and two days later the first machine from the Posen assembly line (w/nr 320003) crashed during its landing run. Tank ordered an immediate enquiry into the two crashes, which were quickly attributed to the acidity of the timber adhesives rotting the plywood structure of the wing.

Prior to the flight of the first prototype, the structure of the Ta 154 had been extensively tested by the towing of the aircraft's fuselage through water at progressively higher speeds. These trials, carried out by the Graf Zeppelin research station in the Alatsee lake in Bavaria, proved very successful. However, shortly after production of the Ta 154A–1 began, the factory that had produced the special adhesives needed, the Goldmann plant at Wuppertal, had been destroyed in an RAF bombing attack. Therefore a new adhesive

Top right: The all-wood Ta 154 V1 was powered by a pair of Jumo 211 engines in annular cowlings.

Bottom right: The Ta 154 V2 undergoing vibration tests prior to completion.

had to be substituted, and it was this that proved to have such a disastrous effect on the wooden structure of the aircraft.

These difficulties led the RLM to have serious doubts about the whole Ta 154 project and when a prototype crashed after an engine fire, they decided to abandon the whole programme. Work was also abandoned on the Ta 154B, C and D and Ta 254 projects which were then under consideration. The Ta 154C was to be powered by Jumo 213A engines and have a bubble canopy and twin ejector seats. The Ta 254 is described in the project section.

In January 1945 the few Ta 154A–1s completed were fitted with FuG 218 *Neptun* variable frequency radar and used for a short time by I./NJG 3 based at Stade. No reports have survived of the machine having been met in combat, and it is likely that the few Ta 154s were quickly replaced by Ju 88Gs.

Apart from being used in its intended rôle, six Ta 154A–0s were modified as lower components for the *Mistel* combination aircraft. Receiving the designation Ta 154A–2/U3, each aircraft carried a 2,000kg (4,410lb) explosive charge in the nose and a Fw 190A–8/U3 fighter mounted above. The two aircraft were to take-off together, and on reaching an enemy bomber formation, the Ta 154 was to be aimed at its centre by the pilot of the Fw 190 and jettisoned. After reaching this position the Ta 154 was to be exploded by remote control. Trials were carried out with the combination by the Junkers test pilot, Horst Lux, but proved unsuccessful.

Specification (Ta 154A–1)

POWERPLANTS	2 × 1,750hp Jumo 213E in-lines
SPAN	16.00m (52ft 6in)
LENGTH	12.10m (39ft 8½in)
HEIGHT	3.50m (11ft 5¾in)
WEIGHT EMPTY	6,405kg (14,123lb)
WEIGHT LOADED	8,250kg (18,191lb)
MAX SPEED	640km/h (398mph)
SERVICE CEILING	10,700m (35,105ft)
NORMAL RANGE	1,365km (848 miles)

Known alternatively as the Ta 154 V3 or A–O3/U1, this prototype was fitted with full radar equipment, armament and two Jumo 213 engines.

A slightly damaged Ta 154A–1 night fighter found after the end of the war in Germany.

Ta 183

Late in 1942 Focke-Wulf's project office, led by Ludwig Mittelhuber, began work on a series of fighter projects to be powered by one of the new turbojet engines then under intensive development. Several of the early designs were to employ a number of Fw 190 components, but by 1943 proposals were crystallising around the completely new *Projekt* VII, unofficially known as the '*Flitzer*' (Madcap).

The Fw P VII bore a remarkable resemblance to the British de Havilland Vampire, being a mid-wing monoplane with a short fuselage nacelle and twin tail booms supporting a high set tailplane. The fighter was to be powered either by a Jumo 004 or HeS O11 turbojet with an auxiliary rocket motor mounted beneath. An armament of two 20mm MG 151/20 and two 30mm MK 108 cannon was proposed initially, these to be replaced at a later stage by four of the new and much faster firing MG 213 weapons then under development.

A mock-up and some sub-assemblies were completed for the '*Flitzer*' before work switched to the much more advanced *Huckebein* project. Named after a mythical raven, the *Huckebein* owed much to the research work carried out by Hans Multhopp on the swept back wing.

Two basic projects were considered, the first having a short barrel-like fuselage with a shoulder mounted wing swept back at a 40 degree angle. The long slender fin and rudder was swept at a 60 degree angle with the tailplane mounted at the apex. A fully retractable nosewheel undercarriage was proposed and an armament of two or four 30mm MK 108 cannon was to be carried.

The second project was for a less aerodynamically refined design with a slimmer fuselage, more conventional tail surfaces and wings swept back at an angle of 32 degrees. Both projects were to feature an all-metal semi-monocoque fuselage with wood and plywood covered flying surfaces. A single 2,860lb thrust Heinkel Hirth HeS 011A composite diagonal and axial flow turbojet was to power both designs, which were also to have full cabin pressurisation.

At the end of 1944 *Oberst* Ernst Kneymeyer, Chief of Technical Air Armament, instigated the emergency fighter competition which called for a single-engined jet fighter to supplement and eventually replace the Me 262. Blohm und Voss, Focke-Wulf, Heinkel, Junkers and Mes-

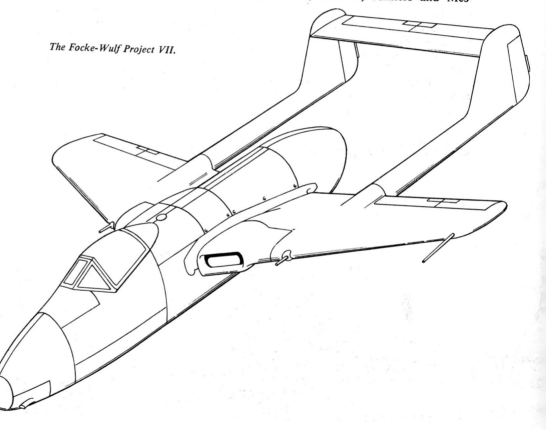

The Focke-Wulf Project VII.

serschmitt all submitted proposals for consideration, a conference being held on February 27th–28th, 1945 to make a final choice. However it was not until the middle of March that Focke-Wulf's first *Huckebein* proposal was finally preferred, receiving the RLM designation Ta 183.

Intensive detailed design work began on the Ta 183 in the spring of 1945, a batch of sixteen prototypes being ordered. The first three of these (the Ta 183 V1 to V3) were to be powered by the 1,980lb thrust Jumo 004 engine, pending delivery of the more powerful HeS 011 unit. The Ta 183 V4 to V14 (also designated Ta 183A–0) were to be powered by the HeS 011A engine and the V15 and V16 were static test airframes. It was estimated that 300 aircraft per month would be delivered when production got into its stride, each Ta 183 being produced in 2,500 manhours.

Despite the intensive work carried out on the Ta 183, construction of the first prototype did not commence before the end of the war in Europe. However, it was certainly one of the most advanced German fighter projects, and one that would have posed severe problems to the Allies had the war continued.

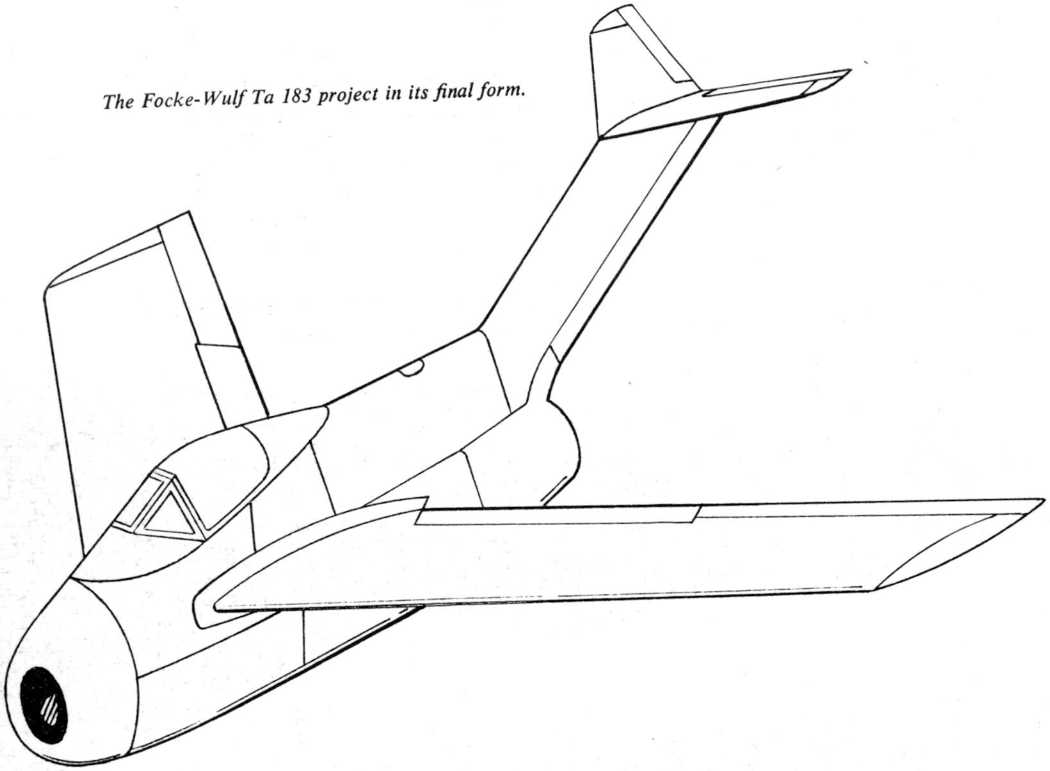

The Focke-Wulf Ta 183 project in its final form.

Specification (Flitzer)

POWERPLANT	1 × 1,300kg (2,860lb) thrust HeS 011A turbojet and 1 × 1,700kg (3,748lb) thrust Walter HWK 509 rocket
SPAN	8.00m (26ft 3in)
LENGTH	10.55m (34ft 7¼in)
HEIGHT	2.35m (7ft 8½in)
WEIGHT LOADED	4,750kg (10,472lb)
MAX SPEED	830km/h (506mph)

(Ta 183 V4)

POWERPLANT	1 × 1,300kg (2,860lb) thrust HeS 011A turbojet
SPAN	10.00m (32ft 9¾in)
LENGTH	9.40m (30ft 10in)
WEIGHT EMPTY	2,830kg (6,241lb)
WEIGHT LOADED	4,300kg (9,481lb)
MAX SPEED	955km/h (593mph)
SERVICE CEILING	14,000m (45,920ft)
NORMAL RANGE	1,300km (808 miles)

Rotating Wing Aircraft

During the early 1930s, Heinrich Focke acquired a licence to build the Cierva C 19 and C 30 autogyros. This helped to stimulate Focke's interest in rotorcraft and eventually led him, in 1933, to resign as Technical Director of Focke-Wulf. Just afterwards, with the assistance of the famous aerobatic pilot, Gerd Achgelis, he formed a specialised rotorcraft company known as the Focke-Achgelis GmbH.

Even before he had formed the new company, Focke had worked on the design of a helicopter, that is an aircraft deriving its lift and propulsion from a horizontally revolving rotor, rather than an autogyro which is virtually a conventionally propelled aircraft with a rotating wing. His Fw 61 (actually built by Focke-Achgelis) was one of the world's first successful helicopters. It was followed by the Fa 223 *Drache* military helicopter and the advanced Fa 284 'flying crane' project.

C 19 Don Quichote

As previously described, Heinrich Focke set up a separate research laboratory within the Focke-Wulf Flugzeugbau AG in 1931 to study the design and construction of rotating wing aircraft. Later in the year, he acquired a licence to build the C 19 Mk.IV autogyro designed by the Spanish pioneer, Don Juan de la Cierva.

The Cierva C 19–IV had a short fuselage constructed of welded steel tube with fabric covering, above which was mounted a pylon carrying a cantilever three-bladed rotor. For the first time initial rotation of the rotor was achieved by the Pitcairn Autogyro Company's clutch drive mechanism, the old slipstream deflection method being abandoned. The low-wing was of broad chord and featured up-turned tips and like the monoplane stabiliser, was constructed of wood with plywood covering. The wide track mainwheels were equipped with Bendix brakes, and a fixed tailskid was positioned below, the rear fuselage.

The Focke-Wulf built C 19–IV was named *Don Quichote* after the legendary Spanish hero and was powered by an 80hp Siemens Sh 11 seven-cylinder radial. Its first flight made in June 1932, led Focke-Wulf to the licence construction of the more advanced Cierva C 30 *Heuschrecke*.

Specification

POWERPLANT	1 × 80hp Siemens Sh 11 radial
ROTOR DIAMETER	10.36m (34ft 0in)
LENGTH	6.92m (22ft 8½in)
HEIGHT	2.82m (9ft 3in)
WEIGHT EMPTY	520kg (1,157lb)
WEIGHT LOADED	705kg (1,555lb)
MAX SPEED	155km/h (96mph)
SERVICE CEILING	2,500m (8,202ft)

The Focke-Wulf C 19 Don Quichote autogyro was based on the Cierva C 19.

C 30 Heuschrecke

The Cierva C 30 was a development of the C 19 which was fitted with a large tripod pylon carrying a faired, tilting rotor head. The wing was completely removed and replaced by a large tailplane with up-turned tips to counteract torque. Control was achieved by tilting the rotor itself by means of a large lever positioned above the pilot's cockpit. The fixed undercarriage was braced to the nose of the autogyro; a large fin was mounted below the rear fuselage and the rotor blades could be folded back to facilitate storage.

Cierva himself made the first flight of the autogyro in April 1933, and soon afterwards Focke-Wulf acquired a licence to build the machine as the C 30 *Heuschrecke* (Grasshopper). The Focke-Wulf built variant was powered by a 140hp Siemens Sh 14a seven-cylinder radial engine and a batch of thirty were built mainly for private ownership.

Heinrich Focke's pre-occupation with rotating aircraft led to a deep sense of disquiet amongst the directors of the company. Eventually, in 1933, Focke decided to resign as technical director of Focke-Wulf to become head of the newly created Focke-Achgelis rotorcraft company.

Specification

POWERPLANT	1 × 140hp Siemens Sh 14a radial
ROTOR DIAMETER	11.28m (37ft 0in)
LENGTH	5.91m (19ft 4¾in)
HEIGHT	3.37m (11ft 0⅔in)
WEIGHT EMPTY	574kg (1,256lb)
WEIGHT LOADED	820kg (1,808lb)
MAX SPEED	160km/h (99mph)
SERVICE CEILING	2,400m (7,874ft)
NORMAL RANGE	350km (217 miles)

Focke-Wulf built about thirty Cierva C 30 autogyros under licence as the Heuschrecke (Grasshopper).

Fw 61

Whilst it is generally accepted that the Wright Brothers built and flew the first successful heavier-than-air aeroplane, the credit for the invention of the helicopter is open to dispute. During the early fifteenth century, the Venetian scientist and painter, Leonardo da Vinci, had designed a helicopter, but the first practical design was that of the Frenchman, Louis Breguet. Soon after the testing of the Breguet–Dorand machine, a much more advanced design was built by *Prof* Heinrich Focke, the Fw 61.

Focke began work on a scale model of the helicopter as early as 1932, but a period of four years elapsed before the machine was flown. Designated Fw 61 V1, the prototype made its first free flight of 28 seconds on June 26th, 1936 with Ewald Rohlfs at the controls. To conserve weight, the helicopter was initially flown without fabric covering, but after successful trials, the undercarriage was considerably modified, the fuselage enclosed and the registration D–EBVU applied.

The Fw 61 employed the fuselage, fin and rudder of the Fw 44 *Stieglitz*, but in place of wings, two large tubular steel outriggers were positioned on either side of the fuselage, each carrying a three-bladed rotor. A single 160hp Siemens Sh 14a radial engine was mounted in the nose of the aircraft, driving the rotors in opposite directions via a complicated system of gearing and shafts. The conventional propeller was replaced by a small cooling fan, and the cyclic pitch of the rotor blades could be adjusted to provide longitudinal and directional control. Lateral control was achieved by simultaneously increasing and decreasing the angle of each rotor, the differential thus created improving lift on the desired side. A single open cockpit was provided for the pilot, and an unusual feature was the positioning of the small horizontal stabiliser above the fin and rudder.

In May 1937, the Fw 61 made its first autorotative landing and during June 25th–26th, the Focke-Achgelis test pilot, Ewald Rohlfs, established a number of FAI records for helicopters. These included an altitude of 2,439m (8,001.95ft); an endurance of 1hr, 20min, 49sec; a distance of 80.604km (50.085 miles) in a straight line; a distance of 122.553km (76.151 miles) over a closed circuit and a speed of 16.40km/h (10.19mph).

Following interest in the helicopter by the Luftwaffe, *Dipl Ing* Karl Francke, chief test pilot of the Rechlin experimental centre and Hanna Reitsch, the celebrated aviatrix, both flew the Fw 61 in September 1937. On October 25th, Hanna Reitsch established a new distance record of 108.974km (67.713 miles) in a straight line. Fraulein Reitsch achieved a more amazing feat in February 1938, when she demonstrated the Fw 61 *inside* the huge Deutschlandhalle in Berlin during the International Automobile Exhibition. This magnificent technical achievement apparently created little impression on the Berlin audience who preferred the various circus acts!

A second prototype was completed in 1937, the Fw 61 V2 (D–EKRA) being generally similar to the first aircraft. On June 20th, 1938 Karl Bode established a third straight line distance record of 230.348km (143.131 miles) and nine days later an altitude of 3,427m (11,243.44ft) was attained. The Hungarian designer, von Asboth, violently contested these records, claiming that the Fw 61 was an autogyro and not a helicopter. As the machine possessed no airscrew, it is difficult to credit his claim.

Specification (Fw 61 V1)

POWERPLANT	1 × 160hp Siemens Sh 14a radial
ROTOR DIAMETER	7.00m (22ft 11¾in)
LENGTH	7.29m (23ft 11in)
WEIGHT EMPTY	800kg (1,760lb)
WEIGHT LOADED	953kg (2,100lb)
MAX SPEED	123km/h (76mph)
SERVICE CEILING	2,410m (7,900ft)
NORMAL RANGE	230km (143 miles)

The Focke-Wulf Fw 61 V1 D–EBVU helicopter preparing for take-off.

Hanna Reitsch demonstrates the Fw 61 V2 during a Nazi Party rally at Nuremburg.

Fw 186

During the autumn of 1935, the RLM issued a requirement for a light transport and liaison aircraft with short take-off and landing characteristics. The specification was drawn-up around the remarkable Fieseler Fi 156 *Storch* which was already under construction, but three other companies submitted designs for consideration. These were Messerschmitt with the Bf 163, Siebel with the Si 201 and later Focke-Wulf with the Fw 186.

The Fw 186, which was designed by *Dipl Ing* Kosel, was a development of the Cierva C 30 autogyro which Focke-Wulf had already built under licence. It was powered by a single 240hp Argus As 10C engine and could carry a crew of two in a neatly streamlined fuselage. The three-bladed rotor was mounted above a single pylon and an extensively braced wide-track undercarriage was fitted.

Only one prototype of the autogyro was completed, this aircraft, the Fw 186 V1 D–ISTQ, flying for the first time in 1938. By this time the Fi 156 had already reached the Luftwaffe and the Fw 186 was abandoned.

Specification

POWERPLANT   1 × 240hp Argus As 10C in-line

No dimensions, weight or performance figures available.

Fa 266 Hornisse

The success of the Fw 61 led Focke-Achgelis to develop in 1938, a six-passenger helicopter for possible use on feeder services by Lufthansa. Designated Fa 266 *Hornisse* (Hornet), the machine was basically an enlarged Fw 61 powered by a single 1,000hp Bramo 323 radial positioned amidships driving two large contra-rotating rotors, each mounted on a steel tube outrigger. Whilst the fin and rudder were entirely conventional in appearance, the tailplane was unusual in being mounted on top of the fin and braced by single struts.

Following the completion of the Fa 266 V1 (D–OCEB) during the summer of 1939, the prototype undertook 100 hours of ground trials before making a series of tethered hovering flights. However, before the helicopter could make its first free flight, it was redesignated as the prototype of the Fa 223 *Drache*.

Specification

(*Similar to the Fa 223.*)

Left: *Only one Fw 186 autogyro was completed.*

Fa 223 Drache

The Fa 223 *Drache* (Dragon) was merely a redesignation of the Fa 266 *Hornisse* helicopter intended for military rather than civilian use. The prototype, which was in fact a redesignation of the Fa 266 V1 (D–OCEB), made its first free flight in August 1940. On October 28th, the Fa 223 V1 attained a record altitude of 23,294ft with Karl Bode at the controls. Trials held at Rechlin experimental station credited the *Drache* with a maximum speed of 115.5mph, considerably in excess of any other contemporary helicopter.

The second prototype, the Fa 223 V2 (D–OGAW) embodied several improvements over the first aircraft, the variant being groomed to establish a new helicopter performance record, a speed of 137mph being anticipated. At one stage, the Fa 223 V2 was fitted with two-bladed rotors, but these did not prove satisfactory, and a return was made to the original three-blade type. Unfortunately the second prototype was destroyed in a bombing attack before its full potential could be realised.

The fuselage of the *Drache* was constructed of welded steel tube, and comprised four separate sections. An extensively glazed nose was provided for the pilot and observer, behind which was positioned a fabric covered freight compartment with an access door in the starboard side. The duralumin covered fuselage centre section was occupied by the 1,000hp Bramo 323Q–3 nine-cylinder radial engine together with its associated cooling fan and gearbox. Aft of the engine compartment was a fabric covered rear fuselage section which faired neatly into the conventional fin and rudder. Above this was a small braced tailplane which could be adjusted for longitudinal trimming.

On either side of the fuselage were mounted two welded tubular steel outriggers, above each of which was fitted a three-blade rotor. Each rotor blade comprised a steel tube to which was attached a series of wooden ribs, the whole covered with a mixture of plywood and fabric. The counter-rotating rotors were inclined inwards at an angle of 4½ degrees and tilted slightly forwards. A nosewheel undercarriage was fitted, with hydraulic brakes operated from the rudder pedals provided for the mainwheels.

In 1942, official acceptance trials resulted in an order being placed for one hundred Fa 223E production models. Developed from the first two prototypes, the Fa 223E was a pure military variant, carrying as standard equipment a 7.9mm MG 15

The second prototype of the Drache *helicopter was the Fa 223 V2 D–OGAW*

machine-gun in the fuselage nose, FuG radio equipment and a FuG 101 radio altimeter.

Several rôles were envisaged for the Fa 223, including that of reconnaissance, rescue, cargo carrying and anti-submarine. For the rescue rôle, an electrically-operated winch was mounted behind the cockpit, operating through the floor. This was supplemented by a hand-held camera for reconnaissance duties, together with a 66 Imp gallon jettisonable fuel tank. For anti-submarine work, the helicopter could carry two 550lb bombs, although torpedo dropping trials proved unsuccessful.

Perhaps the most important task which the Fa 223 was to undertake was that of transporting bulky stores. A special load-carrying beam was mounted inside the fuselage and used to suspend weights of up to 2,820lb. The load could be picked up or set down without the helicopter landing, a special electrically-operated quick release hook being actuated by the pilot. Stores carried during trials included a military staff car and a disassembled Fieseler *Storch* reconnaissance aircraft.

The initial order for 100 Focke-Achgelis helicopters included thirty pre-production Fa 223E–0s to be built at the company's Hoyenkamp factory. In the event, only ten of these were completed before the plant was destroyed by Allied bombing. Production switched to a new factory at Laupheim, but six of the eight helicopters completed were destroyed in another bombing attack in July 1944. A third helicopter assembly line was established near Berlin with a capacity for 400 aircraft per month, but only one other *Drache* was completed before the end of the war.

The Fa 223 demonstrates its capabilities by lifting a Kübelwagen *scout car high into the air.*

Two Focke-Achgelis Fa 223s were completed in Czechoslovakia after the war.

Only a few Fa 223s were used operationally. A machine was intended to assist in the rescue of Benito Mussolini from his mountain prison in September 1943, but was declared unserviceable at the last moment. The only Luftwaffe squadron to operate helicopters was *Transportstaffel 40* at Ainring which was equipped with three Fa 223s and three Flettner Fl 282s in April 1945.

After the end of the war, two Fa 223s were captured intact, one becoming the first helicopter to be flown across the English Channel. Professor Focke assisted the French SNCA du Sud Est company to rebuild a Fa 223 from salvaged components under the designation SE-3000, and two machines were built in Czechoslovakia. Also assembled from salvaged components, the two machines were completed during the winter of 1945/46 under the designation VR-1.

Specification (Fa 223E)

POWERPLANT	1 × 1,000hp Bramo 323Q-3 radial
ROTOR DIAMETER	12.00m (39ft 4½in)
LENGTH	12.25m (40ft 2¼in)
HEIGHT	4.36m (14ft 3½in)
WEIGHT EMPTY	3,180kg (7,000lb)
WEIGHT LOADED	3,860kg (8,500lb)
MAX SPEED	176km/h (109mph)
SERVICE CEILING	2,010m (6,600ft)
NORMAL RANGE	700km (435 miles)

(The performance figures given above are those of a British evaluation report. Other figures differ considerably.)

Fa 224 Libelle

Parallel with the development of the Fa 266 *Hornisse* helicopter for Lufthansa, Focke-Achgelis produced a project for a two-seat sports helicopter under the designation Fa 224 *Libelle* (Dragonfly). The Fa 224 was basically a development of the experimental Fa 61 to be powered by a 270hp Argus As 10E eight-cylinder in-line engine mounted in the nose. The twin three-bladed rotors were to be driven via a system of gears and shafts, and provision was to be made for a crew of two seated side-by-side. Estimated performance figures included a maximum speed of 99mph (160km/h) and a vertical climb rate of 295ft/min (90m/min). With the beginning of World War II, development of the Fa 224 was abandoned.

The first helicopter to fly across the English Channel was this Fa 223 captured by British forces.

Fa 225

On May 10th, 1940 German forces captured the Belgian fort of Eben Emael by the surprise use of troop-carrying gliders. The aircraft which took part in the operation, the DFS 230, had been developed in secret and demonstrated before German army officers as early as 1937. One major drawback of the glider was its inability to land in confined spaces.

Therefore, in 1942, the fuselage of a standard DFS 230 was taken from the production line and fitted with a three-bladed rotor from a Fa 223 *Drache* helicopter mounted above a large pylon. Designated Fa 225, the hybrid also differed from the DFS 230 in having a wheeled undercarriage to absorb the higher landing shocks anticipated with the machine. Built of welded steel tube with fabric covering and carrying a crew of two and eight troops, the Fa 225 was tested behind a Ju 52/3m towplane during 1943.

Although capable of landing in under 18m (59ft), the towing and approach speeds of the Fa 225 were much lower than those of the DFS 230, thus rendering it much more vulnerable to enemy fighters. As far as is known, only one prototype of the Fa 225 was completed.

Specification
ROTOR DIAMETER	12.00m (39ft 4½in)
LENGTH	11.24m (36ft 10½in)
WEIGHT LOADED	2,000kg (4,400lb)
TOWING SPEED	190km/h (118mph)

Right: The Fa 225 was basically the fuselage of a DFS 230 glider with the rotor of a Fa 223 mounted above it on a large pylon.

Fa 284

Undoubtedly the most ambitious German wartime helicopter project was the Focke-Achgelis Fa 284. The Fa 284 was probably the first true 'flying crane' design; that is a helicopter intended specifically to transport heavy loads suspended beneath its belly.

The Fa 284 was a large metal lattice work structure with two large outriggers mounted on either side. A 1,600hp BMW 801 fourteen-cylinder air-cooled radial engine was mounted in each outrigger, driving a three-bladed rotor via the usual complicated system of gearing and shafts. The rear part of the fuselage was fabric covered and a conventional tailplane and fin were braced to this structure. A large mainwheel was fixed beneath each outrigger and a small tailwheel added below the rear fuselage. The pilot and co-pilot were seated in an extensively glazed cabin positioned above and just behind the open lattice work of the fuselage.

A large load of up to 7 metric tons (15,435lb) was eventually intended to be suspended below the belly of the aircraft, this being over half the helicopter's gross weight! Work on the Fa 284 was held up, and eventually abandoned, because of the difficulties associated with the production of the large bevel gears needed for the project. The substitute project for coupling two Fa 223 helicopters together was abandoned at a later stage.

Specification (estimated)
POWERPLANTS	2 × 1,600hp BMW 801 radials
ROTOR DIAMETER	17.83m (58ft 6in)
LENGTH	13.72m (45ft 0in)
WEIGHT EMPTY	8,100kg (17,860lb)
WEIGHT LOADED	12,000kg (26,460lb)
CRUISING SPEED	208km/h (129mph)
ABSOLUTE CEILING	6,350m (20,828ft)
NORMAL RANGE	400km (248 miles)

Fa 330 Bachstelze

During World War II, both Germany and Japan developed small reconnaissance aircraft capable of operating from submarines. The development of such aircraft was encouraged by the difficulties experienced in attempting to seek out and shadow enemy shipping from a submarine lying low in the water.

After abandoning the tiny collapsible Arado Ar 231 monoplane, Germany turned to a much more radical solution to her U-boat reconnaissance aircraft problem, ordering the Focke-Achgelis Fa 330 tethered rotor kite. The Fa 330 *Bachstelze* (Wagtail) comprised a framework of two steel tubes mounted at right angles to each other. On the horizontal tube was mounted a small instrument panel, a control column, the pilot's seat and a fabric covered welded steel tube tail fin and horizontal stabiliser. The vertical member, which was welded to the horizontal tube just behind the pilot's

seat, carried a large three-bladed rotor. Most aircraft were fitted with a simple steel tube skid undercarriage, although the training version was fitted with twin braced oleo legs each carrying a small wheel, and a simple tailskid.

Following the completion of a few Fa 330A–0s, about 200 A–1 production aircraft were built by the Weserflugzeugwerke* at Hoyenkamp near Bremen which also constructed Fw 190 fuselages and the Fa 223 *Drache* helicopter. Training on the Fa 330 was given initially in a wind tunnel at Chalais Meudon in France although the machine proved very easy to handle. The first aircraft were probably delivered during the middle of 1942.

The Fa 330 was intended for use aboard the ocean-going Type IX U-boat which had a surface speed of 18 knots and a displacement of 740 tons. It was claimed that after surfacing the Fa 330 could be

* Focke–Achgelis was a subsidiary of the Weserflugzeugwerke.

made ready for operations in seven minutes. The rotor kite was assembled by hand with the aid of spring loaded lugs and clips, and after attaching the 150m (492ft) long towing cable (which included a telephone line) the rotor was started either by hand or by pulling a rope wound around the rotor head. The machine could then ascend to a maximum altitude of 120m (394ft).

After completing each mission, the Fa 330 would slowly be winched back on board the U-boat and the rotor stopped by the use of an expanding drum brake. If an emergency developed in flight, the pilot could jettison the rotor by pulling a small lever above his head, simultaneously releasing the towing cable. The loss of the rotor pulled a parachute from its stowage behind the vertical pylon, which then automatically opened. The pilot then released his safety belt to jettison the remainder of the rotor kite, and descended by parachute in the normal way.

Several Fa 330 rotor-kites were fitted with wheeled undercarriages for training duties.

Left: *A Fa 330 being towed by a German U-boat.*

It is not known how many Fa 330s were used operationally aboard U-boats, although the machine did serve mainly in the Indian Ocean, an example of a submarine carrying the type being U–861. However the machine was far from popular with submarine crews. If an emergency arose while towing the rotor kite, the U-boat had either to dive and leave the pilot to his fate or risk attack on the surface while attempting his recovery. On at least two occasions a Fa 330 was exchanged for a Japanese Yokosuka E14Y1 floatplane, which the German officers considered a much more useful type.

The obvious solution to these problems was the design of a powered version of the Fa 330, but, although this was proposed under the designation Fa 336, no aircraft was completed. The Fa 336 was to be powered by a 60hp piston engine and have a wheeled undercarriage.

Specification (Fa 330A–1)

ROTOR DIAMETER	7.32m (24ft 0in)
LENGTH	4.42m (14ft 6in)
WEIGHT EMPTY	82kg (180lb)
WEIGHT LOADED	150kg (330lb)
MAX AIRSPEED	40km/h (25mph)
TYPICAL AIRSPEED	27km/h (17mph)

Wartime Aircraft Projects

Fw 205

The probable RLM designation for the Focke-Wulf P.03.10025–1006 project, the Fw 205 was a high-speed night and bad weather fighter with swept-back wings and swept-forward tailplane, the two surfaces being joined at approximately one-third wing span. Power was to be provided by a 4,000hp Argus As 413 engine driving contra-rotating pusher propellers.

Fw 206

The Fw 206 was a project for a twin-engined short and medium range airliner designed in 1939 to replace the Fw 58 *Weihe*. A cantilever low-wing monoplane layout was chosen for the design which was to have provision for a crew of three and about 20 passengers.

The wing was to be built in three sections the outer panels having considerable leading edge sweep-back and dihedral. The fuselage was to be of almost circular section, with an enclosed cabin for the pilot and co-pilot in the nose. A fully retractable undercarriage was proposed, the design owing something to that of the Fw 200. Two prototypes were proposed, the Fw 206 V1 powered by two 1,000hp Bramo 323R–2 radials and the V2 with two experimental 1,200hp BMW 800 engines.

Fw 249

The Focke-Wulf P.95 was a project for the large capacity transport capable of carrying 40 metric tons of freight or 400 troops. Possibly receiving the RLM redesignation

Fw 249, the P.95 was a low-wing monoplane with twin fins and rudders to be powered by eight 2,240hp Jumo 222 twenty-four cylinder engines and carry a crew of seven.

Ta 254

The Focke-Wulf Ta 254 was a proposed high-altitude development of the Ta 154 night fighter. It was to have a clear-blown 'bubble' type canopy and a 30 per cent increase in wing area. Two main variants were proposed, the Ta 254A powered by two 1,750hp Jumo 213 engines and the Ta 254B with 1,750hp DB 603 units. Armament was proposed as two 20mm MG 151/20 and two 30mm MK 108 cannon mounted in the nose. The Ta 254A–3 and B–3 differed from the A–1 and B–1 in having MW–50 injection.

Fw 261

Otherwise known as the P.03.10225–06 project, the Fw 261 was a proposal for a long-range bomber. It was a shoulder-wing monoplane with a central fuselage pod, powered by four 1,700hp BMW 801D radials. Each outboard engine nacelle extended into a tail boom which carried a fin and the port or starboard tailplane. A defensive armament of four 30mm, one 20mm and four 15mm cannon and four 13mm machine guns was proposed plus a 3,000kg (6,600lb) bomb load.

Fa 269

The Focke-Achgelis Fa 269 was a project for a convertiplane; that is an aircraft combining the short-take-off advantages of a helicopter with the higher speeds of a fixed-wing aircraft. The Fa 269 was a conventional mid-wing monoplane with a stepped cockpit in the extreme nose, the underpart of which was also glazed. Two engines were mounted in the wings, just beyond mid span, each driving a large pusher airscrew. The shaft of each engine could be pivoted at a point just aft of the wing leading edge so that the airscrew was parallel with the ground. An extremely tall tailwheel undercarriage was provided, the whole retracting into the fuselage.

Because of the complexity of the various systems involved in the design of the Fa 269, the machine was abandoned in 1944. Apart from the fact that a maximum speed of 600km/h (373mph) was anticipated, no other figures are available for the project.

Ta 283

One of the fastest of all Focke-Wulf projects was the Ta 283 ramjet-powered single-seat fighter. It was an all-metal monoplane with a low set wing, the leading edge of which was swept back 45 degrees. The cockpit was positioned in the centre of the fuselage, the canopy being faired into the large swept-back tailfin and rudder, A large Pabst type ramjet engine was mounted at the tip of each swept-back tailplane, an auxiliary Walter rocket providing power for take-off. A fully retractable nosewheel undercarriage was to be provided.

Fw 300

A development of the Fw 200 *Condor*, the Fw 300 was a project for a long-range airliner, produced in parallel with the Fw 206. It was an all-metal cantilever low-wing monoplane with a pressurised cabin for a crew of five and forty passengers. The wing was, like that of the Fw 206, to be built in three sections, the outer panels employing considerable leading-edge sweep-back. The fuselage was a smoothly streamlined structure of completely circular cross section, with two entrance doors in the port side. Four DB 603 in-line engines in annular cowlings were to power the Fw 300, each developing 1,950hp.

A mock-up of the airliner was completed with a beautifully appointed cabin interior, but soon afterwards the design was re-worked as a bomber under the designation Fw 300A. Detailed design work for the bomber proceeded under *Dipl Ing* Banse-

Specification

	Fw 205	Fw 206	Fw 249	Ta 254	Fw 261
SPAN	16.40m (53ft 9⅔in)	27.30m (89ft 6¾in)	58.00m (190ft 3½in)	18.00m (59ft 0½in)	40.00m (131ft 3in)
LENGTH	14.20m (46ft 7in)	19.60m (64ft 3¼in)	47.00m (154ft 2⅓in)	13.70m (44ft 11⅓in)	26.10m (85ft 7⅔in)
WEIGHT LOADED	9,800kg (21,605lb)	10,600kg (23,373lb)	112,000kg (246,960lb)	11,500kg (25,357lb)	53,500kg (117,967lb)
MAX SPEED	840km/h (522mph)	415km/h (258mph)	490km/h (305mph)	740km/h (460mph)	450km/h (280mph)
SERVICE CEILING				10,520m (34,518ft)	
NORMAL RANGE			1,500km (932 miles)	1,440km (895 miles)	8,500km (5,282 miles)

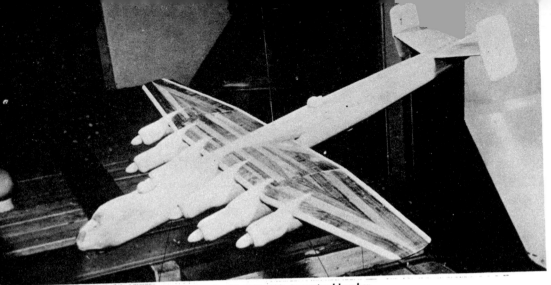

A wind tunnel model of the Focke-Wulf Ta 400 six-engined bomber.

mir, production of the prototype Fw 300 V1 being switched to the French SNCASO factory near Paris. In the event, neither the Fw 300A bomber nor Fw 300B reconnaissance aircraft were completed.

Ta 400

After the USA entered the war at the end of 1941, the RLM issued a revised specification for their *Amerika-Bomber*; an aircraft capable of attacking New York from European bases. The revised specification, which called for a machine with six engines and increased defensive armament, resulted in three separate projects, the Messerschmitt Me 264B, the Junkers Ju 390 and the Focke-Wulf Ta 400.

The projected Ta 400 was a mid-wing monoplane of all-metal stressed skin construction with provision for a crew of six in two separate pressurised cabins. The wing was to be built in three sections, the outer panels having both leading and trailing edge taper. The fuselage was to be a circular monocoque structure and twin fins and rudders were to be fitted. Defensive armament was projected as two 20mm MG 151/20 cannon in each of five remotely-controlled gun barbettes. A maximum bomb load of 10,000kg (22,000lb) was proposed.

A number of Ta 400 variants were projected, the original having a stepped cockpit and six BMW 801D fourteen-cylinder radial engines, each developing 1,700hp for take-off. Later versions had a smoothly streamlined nose with considerable glazing, the final proposal introducing two 800kg (1,980lb) thrust Junkers Jumo 004B turbojets mounted beneath the outboard engine nacelles.

Detailed design work on the Ta 400 began early in 1943, at a Focke-Wulf controlled technical group at Chatillon in France. A number of companies in Germany, France and Italy were allocated contracts for the development and construction of various component parts for the Ta 400, but despite promise, it was dropped in favour of the Junkers Ju 390.

Specification	Ta 283	Fw 300	Ta 400	Triebflügel
SPAN	7.97m (26ft 1¾in)	46.20m (151ft 7in)	45.80m (150ft 3¼in)	11.50m (37ft 8¾in)*
LENGTH	11.81m (38ft 9in)	31.00m (101ft 8½in)	28.70m (94ft 2in)	9.15m (30ft 0in)
WEIGHT LOADED	5,380kg (11,863lb)	47,500kg (104,737lb)	60,000kg (132,300lb)	5,175kg (11,410lb)
MAX SPEED	1,125km/h (699mph)	525km/h (326mph)	725km/h (450mph)	1,000km/h (621mph)
SERVICE CEILING	10,000m (32,811ft)	9,600m (31,500ft)		14,000m (45,920ft)
NORMAL RANGE	690km (429 miles)	8,200km (5,095 miles)	5,000km (3,107 miles)	650km (404 miles)

* The span of the Triebflügel project is actually the rotor diameter.

Triebflügel

Perhaps the most remarkable of a number of interesting projects produced by Focke-Wulf was the *Triebflügel* (Thrust Wing) VTOL fighter developed in September 1944. The fuselage of the project was to stand vertically on the ground, supported by a small wheel at the tip of four tailfins. A large central wheel, enclosed by a clamshell door when not in use, was to support the main weight of the fuselage. Lift and thrust was to be provided by three rotating wings, each of which was driven by a 840kg (1,850lb) thrust Ramjet engine mounted at the tip. Rotation of the wings was to be started by the firing of three 300kg (660lb) thrust rockets.

The pilot was to be seated in the extreme nose of the aircraft beneath a small clear-blown canopy. Control was to be effected by small movable surfaces at the rear of each tailfin. An armament of two 20mm MG 151/20 and two 30mm MK 108 cannon was proposed, to be carried beneath the pilot's position. The Pabst type ramjets were successfully tested at speeds of up to Mach 0.9 in the Brunswick wind tunnel, but the project was too advanced to see fruition.

Other projects

Apart from those projects just described, Focke-Wulf produced a multitude of interesting designs during the war years. These were normally recognised by a most complicated series of figures, often incorporating the engine type number. There were so many projects that, even if all their features had survived, they would be impossible to describe in a work of this nature. However, it may be of interest to describe briefly some of the more advanced projects.

Projekt 82114 was for a parasol wing dive bomber to compete with the Junkers Ju 87. It was a two-seater with an enclosed cockpit, a fixed undercarriage and a DB 600 engine. The Focke-Wulf Projekt 03.10224 was for a four- or six-engined bomber somewhat similar to the Ta 400, and the P.03.10251–13 was a night and bad-weather fighter. Designed to be powered by a 2,500hp Jumo 222 engine mounted as a pusher and two 800kg (1,760lb) thrust BMW 003 turbojets slung under the wings, the P.03.10251–13 project was to feature swept wings and a cruciform tail similar to that used earlier by the Dornier Do 335.

A considerable amount of work was carried out by the Focke-Wulf design office on the 1000 × 1000 × 1000 bomber projects. Three basic projects were considered, all designed to carry a 1,000kg (2,210lb) load over a distance of 1,000km (621 miles) at a speed of 1,000km/h. Projekt A was for a neat mid-wing monoplane with swept flying surfaces, bearing a passing resemblance to the American B–47 Stratojet. It was to be powered by two HeS 011 turbojets mounted beneath the wings. Projekt B was an all-wing design built in three sections. The centre triangular section incorporated a small crew nacelle and twin HeS 011 turbojets, the outer panels being swept back and featuring underslung fins at each tip. Projekt C was an ugly design with square section wings and tail, a bulky fuselage and a HeS 011 turbojet slung beneath each wing.

VAK 191B

In 1964 the Luftwaffe and Italian Air Force requested the development of a single-seat vertical take-off strike and reconnaissance aircraft to replace the Fiat G.91R. Four designs competed in the VAK (*Vertical-Aufklärungs-und-Kampfeinsitzer*) 191 contest; the Hawker Siddeley Kestrel (VAK 191A), the VFW 1262 (VAK 191B), the EWR 340 (VAK 191C) and the Fiat G.95/4 (VAK 191D). Eventually the VFW 1262 project was chosen as winner of the contest and an order was placed for three prototypes.

The VFW 1262, or VFW/Fokker VAK 191B as it is now known, is a shoulder-wing monoplane with short stubby flying surfaces and a clear blown canopy mounted just behind the nose. It is powered by a single 4,630kg (10,207lb) thrust Rolls-Royce/MTU RB 193–12 vectored thrust turbojet and two 2,530kg (5,578lb) thrust Rolls-Royce/MTU RB 162–81 vertical lift engines. The VAK 191B has fully retractable mainwheels mounted in tandem balanced by a tiny outrigger wheel at each wing tip, but no armament is fitted.

After protracted development, the first prototype, the VAK 191B V1 was rolled out on April 24th, 1970 and began a series of tethered flight trials early in 1971. The first free flight was made at Bremen on September 10th, 1971, being joined on October 2nd by the second prototype. All three aircraft are due to be handed over to the German government for use as systems test vehicles in connexion with the Panavia multi-rôle combat aircraft (MRCA) project now under development. A fully operational version, the VAK 191B Mk 2 has also been proposed, with increased wing area and four pylons for underwing stores.

Specification (VAK 191B V1)

POWERPLANTS	1 × 4,630kg (10,207lb) thrust RB 193–12 and 2 × 2,530kg (5,578lb) thrust RB 162–81 turbojets
SPAN	6.16m (20ft 2½in)
LENGTH	14.72m (48ft 3½in)
HEIGHT	4.29m (14ft 1in)
WEIGHT EMPTY	5,305kg (11,695lb)
WEIGHT LOADED	7,995kg (17,626lb)
MAX SPEED	1,175km/h (730mph)

VFW 614

Apart from being the first German jet airliner, the VFW 614 short-haul design is by far the most promising aircraft under development by the Vereinigte Flugtechnische Werke, successor to the wartime Focke-Wulf and Heinkel companies. It is an all-metal low-wing monoplane with a fully retractable nosewheel undercarriage. The cantilever wing is slightly swept and the airliner is designed to carry 36, 40 or 44 passengers in three alternative configurations.

The VFW 614 was originated by the Weser company in 1961 as a DC–3 replacement under the designation E 614 (the fourth project conceived in 1961). It was designed around two projected Lycoming PLF 1B turbofans, and details were publicly released at the 1963 Paris Air Show as the Weser WFG 614. In 1965 the Lycoming engine was abandoned and VFW (which had been formed from an amalgamation of Weser, Focke-Wulf and Heinkel) were forced to look around for a new power unit. Eventually the Rolls-Royce/SNECMA M 45H engine was chosen for the project, an unusual feature being that they were mounted above the wings.

VFW were fortunate in obtaining the

The VAK 191B which made its first flight on September 10th, 1971.

assistance of the Fokker, Siat, Dowty-Rotol and Belgian Fairey and SABCA companies in the project, and in March 1971 testing of a static airframe began at Lemwerder. The first prototype, the VFW 614 G1 (D-BABA) was rolled out at Bremen on April 5th, 1971 and after taxying trials made its initial flight on July 19th. The second aircraft, the VFW 614 G2 made its first flight on January 14th, 1972 and the company still hope to complete the first production aircraft (the VFW 614 G4) before the end of the year.

At present, VFW/Fokker holds 26 options for the airliner from nine civil companies and the Spanish Air Ministry.

It is hoped that by 1980 the company will be able to sell 350 to 400 VFW 614s.

Specification

POWERPLANTS	2 × 3,410kg (7,510lb) thrust M 45H turbofans
SPAN	21.50m (70ft 6½in)
LENGTH	20.60m (67ft 7in)
HEIGHT	7.84m (25ft 8in)
WEIGHT EMPTY	12,000kg (26,896lb)
WEIGHT LOADED	18,600kg (41,006lb)
MAX SPEED	740km/h (460mph)
CRUISING SPEED	627km/h (390mph)
NORMAL RANGE	630km (391 miles)

The attractive VFW 614 G1 airliner prototype (D-BABA) with its distinctive overwing engine layout.

Some Notes on Aircraft and Unit Designations

After the end of World War I, Focke-Wulf retained the old aircraft designation system which Germany had used throughout the conflict. This included the prefix 'A' for unarmed aircraft, 'GL' for light twin-engined aircraft, 'F' for civil aircraft and 'W' for floatplanes. Additionally, the Focke-Wulf prefix 'S' was used for specialised training aircraft.

When the Nazis came to power in 1933, the RLM rationalised all aircraft designation systems, allocating each design a number from a single progressive list, prefixed by '8'. Thus the Focke-Wulf A 43 became the Fw 43 and the A 44 became the Fw 44 etc. The new RLM numbers were allotted in batches; for example 133 to 134 was used by Bücker, 135 to 144 by Blohm und Voss and 145 to 150 by Gotha. Each aircraft number was prefixed by a two or three letter code indicating the manufacturer of the aircraft. For example: Heinkel used 'He', Focke-Wulf used 'Fw' and Focke-Achgelis 'Fa'. Towards the end of 1942, the part Kurt Tank had played in the design of Focke-Wulf aircraft was recognised when the prefix 'Ta' replaced 'Fw' for all types produced by the company.

The aircraft designation was followed by a letter which identified a major sub-type; eg: the Fw 190A, B, C etc. For more minor modifications a number was used; eg: Fw 189A-1, A-2, A-3 etc. Finally very minor modifications were identified by the letter 'U' and a number; eg: Fw 190D-9/U1. Conversion packs were recognised in a similar manner, but with the letter 'R' replacing 'U'.

All prototypes carried a *Versuchs* (experimental) number, the first prototype of the Focke-Wulf *Uhu* being the Fw 189 V1, the second the Fw 189 V2 and so on. Pre-production aircraft carried the normal suffix letter plus the number 'O'. Thus the Ta 152C–0 was the pre-production aircraft for the 'C' series.

The basic Luftwaffe unit was the *Staffel* or squadron which was normally made up of between nine and twelve aircraft. Three or four *Staffeln* were combined to form a *Gruppe* and three or four *Gruppen* were combined to form a *Geschwader* or wing. *Geschwader* were identified by an Arabic number, *Gruppen* within a *Geschwader* by a Roman numeral. Independent *Gruppen* were identified by an Arabic number as were all *Staffeln*. Each type of unit was prefaced by an abbreviation which identified its rôle. For example the letters 'JG' identified a *Jagdgeschwader* or fighter wing. The designation II./JG 52 identified the second group of fighter wing 52, while the designation 2./JG 52 identified the second squadron of the same wing.

Abbreviations

Aufkl. Gr	*Aufklärungsgruppe*	Reconnaissance group
DFS	*Deutsches Forschungsinstitut für Segelflug*	German research institute for sailplanes
DVL	*Deutsche Versuchsanstalt für Luftfahrt*	German experimental institute for aviation
DLH	*Deutsche Lufthansa*	German airlines. (It should be remembered that the airline was more correctly known as *Deutsche Luft-Hansa* prior to January 1st, 1934. For the sake of continuity the more modern term *Lufthansa* has been used throughout)
(F)	*Fern-*	Long-range
(H)	*Heeres-*	Army co-operation
JG	*Jagdgeschwader*	Fighter wing
Jabo	*Jagdbomber*	Fighter-bomber
KG	*Kampfgeschwader*	Bomber wing
LG	*Lehrgeschwader*	Instructional wing
(N)	*Nah-*	Short-range
NJG	*Nachtjagdgeschwader*	Night fighter wing
Ob.d.L.	*Oberbefehlshaber der Luftwaffe*	High command of the Air Force
RLM	*Reichsluftfahrtministerium*	German Aviation Ministry
SG	*Schlachtgeschwader*	Ground attack wing (second units)
Sch.G	*Schlachtgeschwader*	Ground attack wing (first units)
TG	*Transportgeschwader*	Transport wing
zbV	*zur besonderen Verwendung*	on special employment. (Usually applied to a bomber group operating on transport duties)

Luftwaffe Commissioned Rank Abbreviations

Lt	*Leutnant*	(Pilot Officer)
Oblt	*Oberleutnant*	(Flying Officer)
Hptm	*Hauptmann*	(Flight Lieutenant)
Maj	*Major*	(Squadron Leader)
Oberstlt	*Oberstleutnant*	(Wing Commander)
Oberst	*Oberst*	(Group Captain)
Gen Maj	*General-Major*	(Air Commodore)
Gen Lt	*General-Leutnant*	(Air Vice Marshal)
Gen d Fl	*General der Flieger*	(Air Marshal)
Gen Oberst	*General-Oberst*	(Air Chief Marshal)
Gen Feldm	*General-Feldmarschall*	(Marshal of the Royal Air Force)

Type and Production List

DESIGNATION	AIRCRAFT TYPE	DATE	BUILT FOR (OWNER)	NO. BUILT
A 4	Single-seat experimental monoplane	1911	Focke-Wulf	1
A 5	Single-seat experimental monoplane	1912	Focke-Wulf	1
A 7	Two-seat monoplane trainer	1921	Focke-Wulf	1
A 16	3- or 4-passenger monoplane airliner	1924	Various civil airlines	23
S 1	Two-seat monoplane trainer	1925	—	1 or 2
S 2	Two-seat monoplane trainer	1927	—	1
A 17	8-passenger monoplane airliner	1927	Norddeutsche Luftverkehr and DLH	12
GL 18	Monoplane crew trainer	1926	—	—
F 19	4-seat experimental canard aircraft	1927	DVL	2
A 20	3- or 4-passenger monoplane airliner	1928	Various civil airlines	4
A 21	Photographic reconnaissance aircraft	1928	Hansa Luftbild GmbH	1
GL 22	Monoplane crew trainer	1928	—	—
W 4	Two-seat biplane reconnaissance floatplane	1928	DVS	—
S 24	Two-seat biplane trainer	1928	Private owners	none
G 25	Large transport project	1928	—	1
A 26	8-passenger monoplane airliner	1928	DVL	1
A 28	3- or 4-passenger monoplane airliner	1928	Various civil airlines	5
A 29	8-passenger monoplane airliner	1929	Lufthansa and DVS	5
A 32	6-passenger monoplane airliner	1930	Nordbayerische Verkehrsflug	3
A 33	3-passenger monoplane airliner	1930	Lufthansa and private owners	1
A 36	Monoplane postal aircraft	1931	Lufthansa	1
A 38	8-passenger monoplane airliner	1931	Lufthansa	4
A 39	Two-seat parasol wing reconnaissance aircraft	1931	—	1
A 40	Two-seat parasol wing reconnaissance aircraft	1932	—	1
W 7	Two-seat biplane reconnaissance aircraft	1932		1
A 43	3-seat monoplane taxi aircraft	1932	Norddeutsche Luftverkehr	1
Fw 44	Two-seat biplane trainer	1933	NSFK, Luftwaffe and private owners	—
Fw 47	Two-seat meteorological reconnaissance aircraft	1932	Meteorological research stations	at least 21
S 48	Light transport and trainer project	1931	—	none
Fw 55	Two-seat parasol wing trainer	1933	DVS and private owners	—
Fw 56	Single-seat parasol wing trainer	1933	NSFK and Luftwaffe	about 1,000
Fw 57	3-seat monoplane light bomber	1935	Luftwaffe	1
Fw 58	6-seat communications monoplane	1935	Lufthansa and Luftwaffe	—
Fw 62	Two-seat biplane floatplane	1937	Luftwaffe	2
Fw 159	Single-seat parasol wing fighter	1935	Luftwaffe	3
Fw 187	Single- or two-seat fighter monoplane	1938	Luftwaffe	9
Fw 189	3-seat reconnaissance monoplane	1939	Luftwaffe	835

DESIGNATION	AIRCRAFT TYPE	DATE	BUILT FOR (OWNER)	NO. BUILT
Fw 190	Single-seat monoplane fighter	1939	Luftwaffe	about 19,500
Fw 191	4-seat medium bomber	1942	Luftwaffe	3
Fw 198	Single-seat fighter (See note)	1940	—	—
Fw 200	Airliner and reconnaissance monoplane	1937	Lufthansa and Luftwaffe	—
Ta 152	Single-seat fighter monoplane	1943	Luftwaffe	about 200
Ta 153	Single-seat fighter monoplane	1944	Luftwaffe	1
Ta 154	Two-seat night fighter monoplane	1943	Luftwaffe	about 24
Ta 183	Single-seat swept wing jet fighter	1945	Luftwaffe	none
Fw 205	Night and bad weather fighter project	1944	Luftwaffe	none
Fw 206	Light airliner project	1940	Lufthansa	none
Ta 211	Original designation of Ta 154	1943	Luftwaffe	none
Fw 249	Large transport project	1942	Luftwaffe	none
Fw 261	Long-range bomber project	1944	Luftwaffe	none
Ta 254	Projected development of Ta 154	1944	Luftwaffe	none
Ta 283	Single-seat ramjet fighter monoplane	1944	Luftwaffe	none
Fw 300	Four-engined airliner project	1942	Lufthansa	none
Ta 400	Six-engined bomber project	1943	Luftwaffe	none
Triebflügel	Single-seat VTOL fighter project	1944	Luftwaffe	
C 19	Two-seat autogyro	1932	Focke-Wulf	—
C 30	Two-seat autogyro	1933	Private owners	30
Fw 61	Single-seat experimental helicopter	1936	Luftwaffe	2
Fw 186	Two-seat reconnaissance autogyro	1938	Luftwaffe	1
Fa 266	Twin-rotor helicopter	1939	Lufthansa	none
Fa 223	Twin-rotor military helicopter	1940	Luftwaffe	21
Fa 224	Sports helicopter project	1940	Private owners	none
Fa 225	Rotating wing transport	1942	Luftwaffe	1
Fa 269	Convertiplane fighter project	1941	Luftwaffe	none
Fa 284	Flying crane helicopter project	1942	Luftwaffe	none
Fa 330	Rotating wing reconnaissance aircraft	1942	Kriegsmarine	—
Fa 336	Powered development of Fa 330	1943	Kriegsmarine	none
VAK 191B	Single-seat jet VTOL aircraft	1971	Luftwaffe	3
VFW 614	40-passenger short haul airliner	1971	Various civil airlines	—

NB: The designation 'Fw 198' was invented by the British aviation press during 1940 and referred in fact to a Dutch aircraft, the De Schelde S.21. No such designation as the 'Fw 198' was allocated by the RLM or used by Focke-Wulf.